THE HUNGRY TRAVELLER IN FRANCE

FINE NAPOLÉON

THE HUNGRY TRAVELLER
IN FRANCE

BY

NORMAN DAVEY

JONATHAN CAPE
THIRTY BEDFORD SQUARE
LONDON

FIRST PUBLISHED 1931

JONATHAN CAPE LTD., 30 BEDFORD SQUARE, LONDON
AND 91 WELLINGTON STREET WEST, TORONTO
JONATHAN CAPE & HARRISON SMITH INC.
139 EAST 46TH STREET, NEW YORK

PRINTED IN GREAT BRITAIN BY J. AND J. GRAY, EDINBURGH
PAPER MADE BY JOHN DICKINSON AND CO. LTD.
BOUND BY A. W. BAIN AND CO. LTD.

CONTENTS

	PAGE
FOREWORD	xi

FIRST PART

GASTROGRAPHY

FIRST JOURNEY — DOWN

CHAPTER		PAGE
I.	CHANNEL PORTS	25
II.	BEAUVAIS	34
III.	WITHIN THE ISLAND OF FRANCE	41
IV.	THROUGH THE ORLÉANAIS	49
V.	THE NIVERNAIS AND LOWER BURGUNDY	57
VI.	THE LOWER RHÔNE	66
VII.	PROVENCE	77
VIII.	TOM TIDDLER'S GROUND	86

SECOND JOURNEY — UP

IX.	THE WINTER ROUTE	101
X.	THE ALL-GOLD ROAD	113
XI.	THROUGH THE WAR ZONE	127

THIRD JOURNEY — ACROSS

| XII. | THE VAR | 135 |
| XIII. | FROM SEA TO SEA | 148 |

CONTENTS

FOURTH JOURNEY — ACROSS

CHAPTER		PAGE
XIV.	FROM GUYENNE TO NORMANDY	161

THREE CAPITALS IN GASTRONOMY

XV.	LYON	175
XVI.	MARSEILLE	186
XVII.	BORDEAUX	199

SECOND PART

WINE LIST

XVIII.	CLARET	207
XIX.	BURGUNDY	226
XX.	FRENCH WINES OTHER THAN CLARETS AND BURGUNDIES	238

THIRD PART

SQUATTING

XXI.	THE ENGLISH COLONY	245
XXII.	DOMESTIC ECONOMY	254
XXIII.	ADMONITION	263
	APPENDICES	267
	INDEX	293

LIST OF ILLUSTRATIONS

FINE NAPOLÉON	*Frontispiece*

	PAGE
LE CHICHIS	30
IT IS NOT THE MOMENT TO MAKE GASTRONOMICAL INQUIRIES	52
COMMERCIAL GENTLEMEN KNOW WHERE TO DINE	62
YOU CAN CATCH YOUR OWN FISH	94
A MONTE CARLO IDYLL	98
YOU CAN WEAR PLUS-FOURS ALL THE WAY DOWN	114
A WELCOME AS IN A RAILWAY STATION	120
A PROVENÇAL WORKER	142
LE BRACONNIER	156
LE PASTIS	190
BAD WAITING	200
STILL LIFE IN AIX-EN-PROVENCE	252

MAPS

DEPARTMENTS OF FRANCE	26
CARTE VINICOLE DU DÉPARTEMENT DE LA GIRONDE	208

À MORTON SHAND, QUI CONNAÎT LE VIN :
À MORTON FULLERTON, QUI CONNAÎT LA FINESSE :
A S. D., CHI CAPISCE LA GHIOTTONERIA.

It is good and comely for one to eat and to drink, and to enjoy the good of all his labour.

ECCLESIASTES.

Non minus ingenua est mihi, Marce, gula.

MARTIAL.

They order, said I, this matter better in France.

STERNE.

TO THE HUNGRY TRAVELLER — A FOREWORD

It might well be considered impudent, in these informed days, to advise any man upon what poor Yorick called 'posting through the politer kingdoms of the Globe.' Much has happened since Laurence Sterne started upon his Sentimental Journey. To travel in Europe to-day — and especially to travel in France — is scarcely more than to take a turn or two in the backyard. The railway, the airplane and the motor car have eaten up distances. The motor coach has devastated the country-side. The luxury of foreign travel is no longer a privilege of the wealthy. The amazing advance in mechanical and community transport, the enterprise of tourist agencies, the cheapening of mass-produced cars, has opened up the remotest fastnesses of Europe alike to the shopkeeper and to the artisan, as to the rich and to the retired: whilst Paris and Monte Carlo compete with Brighton and Blackpool in the provision of proletarian delights. The fall of the franc has, above all, made these things to be. To-day it is as cheap (if not cheaper) for the Briton to summer rather in St. Malo than at Margate; and the language difficulty is no impediment in a country where every one speaks English when so desired — as often when not. To instruct even the most innocent of travellers would seem to be a matter of supererogation. The pocket encyclopædias of Messrs. Baedeker, Michelin and others equip the studious with knowledge both intellectual and economic, providing a pabulum alike for the body as for the soul. With agents as reliable and as ubiquitous as those of Messrs. Cook and Lunn, the most feckless can come to but little harm. English newspapers are procurable at almost any bookstall, whilst the activity of Tauchnitz provides reading matter of a less ephemeral sort. English bankers operate in all the principal towns of France and may, sometimes, be persuaded into cashing a cheque at sight. English agencies will convey you in motor cars, let you villas, lend you books, reserve your seats in the theatre; sell you tea, tickets, dogs or whisky, and insure you against fire, burglary, theft, illness, accidents, domestic servants and third-party risks – against anything and everything, in fact, except Casino losses and offences against the Napoleonic Code. English clergymen will exhort you on a Sunday, visit you when sick, comfort you when penitent and bury you when dead from Garavan to Calais. A million or more of us have spent more time than we care to remember in what the Military Cartographer called 'Belgium and a part of France'; and the poorest linguist among us speaks the vernacular (if ever needed) at least badly enough to be understood.

In brief, so widely is the country overrun and so deeply is the community infiltrated by the Anglo-Saxon, that one might well believe that there is nothing left to examine or to explore, and that to attempt either were but an exercise in the commonplace.

Yet, out of all the many millions of English men and women who cross the Channel in a year, I wonder how many know France. I mean the real France. Not the cosmopolitan scrum of the Boulevard of the Italians or the Promenade of the English. Not the Southend jollity of Dinard, the dizzy dash of Deauville, the Britannic snobbery of La Croisette, the international naughtiness of Monaco or bridge and Colonel Bogey in Béarn.

For Calais and Boulogne: Dinard and Deauville: Nice and Cannes and Biarritz are not France. Paris is not France. One might almost say that France is not France. Yet, by the oddest of paradoxes, France is very strictly and peculiarly France: more so to-day, perhaps, than she ever was before. Even Biarritz, which is Basque, and Nice, which is Italian, and Monte Carlo, which is Monagasque, and Paris, which, according to the latest information, is American, are all integral parts of France. But the true France, which is still in the heart of all these strange and exotic places, is more easily to be seen and more comfortably to be enjoyed, away from such boosted and bedizened resorts throughout the quiet and fertile country between the Channel and the Gulf of Lions, the Bay of Biscay and the Alps. For it is to be remembered that France is nearly four times as large as England and Wales and that your tourist (fortunately) is a very unenterprising fellow and rarely scrambles out of the rut that has been worn for him by his predecessors. Within those travelled ways there is little of the real France to be found. You may take a ticket on the Blue Train or land at la Joliette; play golf at Chantilly, tennis at Beaulieu or baccara at the Sporting – or even paint a G.B. at the back of your car – without discovering the least little bit of France. For all such a traveller may find of 'knowledge and improvements,' he may as well have kept his car in England, his money in his pocket and stayed at home. 'Have you been in France?' asked the civil gentleman of Yorick. Yet of the millions of travellers who might answer in the affirmative, I doubt that there are but few who have seen more of France than the Atlantic tourist sees of England in Piccadilly, Shakespeare's Avon, 'Glorious' Devon and the railway company's posters.

And he, at least, speaks – or anyhow understands – English. What the French tourist, ignorant of the idiom, may see in England, I hesitate to conjecture. But there are, in any case, no French tourists in Britain – so it does not matter. In the first place, no man of sense is ready to spend money at five times the rate of that at which he receives it; and secondly, every Frenchman very properly considers his own country the finest in the world, the wine the most delicate, the food the best cooked, the women the most witty, and the language the most elegant. You rarely meet a Frenchman out of France; and, I might add, not often in it. He is of an economic disposition and lives much at home. In Paris, he is nearly extinct, hiding underground in the tube railways, in small cafés behind the Bourse, and for all I know to the contrary (having never been there), in the tomb of Napoleon. At least, the ordinary traveller does not meet him. His hotel-keeper will be a Swiss or an Italian: his waiter a Czech or a Pole: his taxi-driver a Russian: his bar-tender an

FOREWORD

Englishman or an American; and the gentleman who offers him his services as guide an Armenian. As for any others, who administer to his comfort and aid him in his itinerary, they will be either Scots or Jews or (possibly) both. Even the most sanguine traveller will scarcely expect to extract that spirit which is peculiarly French from any one of these. After all, to quote the excellent Yorick once again, 'an Englishman does not travel to see Englishmen': or even such others as the French designate as 'métèques.' The more enterprising of us hope, occasionally, to meet a native.

It is to this traveller that I peculiarly address myself. To such an one who would see something more of France than the particular playgrounds within which his fellow-countrymen are so comfortably (and expensively) segregated. To him who would see something of manners and customs, of food and drink, of ways of life, especially French. I am not concerned here with monuments. They are all in Baedeker. Churches and pictures are well enough in their way; anyhow, most of us have already seen the best of them, and I am now of an age to paraphrase the Great Lexicographer and say, 'one monument is very like another monument; give me men' – or, at least, give me something to eat. And here I come to the Identical of this book, the *fons et origo* of this *opus*: the urge to speak, the itch to write, the necessity in this *historia*. For although I address myself to the Intellectual Traveller: to the Gentle Traveller, in the right sense of that much-abused word: to the Informed Traveller (for I shall presume in him some knowledge of the country and practice in the tongue): to the Understanding Traveller:

to the Curious Traveller: to the Modest Traveller and to the Ingenious Traveller, it is to the Hungry Traveller, and, indeed, to the Thirsty Traveller, that I herewith positively present myself and for whom I most particularly write. Not, be it understood, for the common greedy. Not for gluttons and wine-bibbers; not for him who is alone 'good but to taste sack and drink it' and 'neat and cleanly but to carve a capon and eat it,' but to the Traveller of Taste and Discretion, who will wisely order his meals to the enlivening of his intellect; who is honestly epicure and honourably dilettante: who is old enough to have achieved a palate and young enough to have preserved a digestion: neither crank nor snob, whose head is only perpendicularly above his stomach.

To such an one alone, this little book may, I hope, be of service. To others, less so: for I have, through many happy years spent in this agreeable land of France, met odd Englishmen. There are those, more endowed with wealth than they deserve, who measure entertainment by its cost alone. There are, again, others who seek bodily luxury rather than stomachic content, and are unhappy without private baths and all the paraphernalia of a sanitary perfection. There are Insulars, miserable without brandied whiskies and underdone chops. There are the Eating Snobs and the Drinking Snobs, who eat and drink at cost and inconvenience rather to talk about it afterwards than to enjoy it at the time. There is that quaint creature, the Travelled Snob, who will swallow, with apparent enjoyment, all sorts of oddities, if he, alone, has discovered them. And, lastly, there is the Mean Traveller,

FOREWORD

who, since the franc is nominally worth twopence, expects to budget with it at a penny.

For none of those others are the following pages written. For such as desire solid, and even princely, accommodation and entertainment, the excellent Annual published by the firm of Michelin is without rival. For those seeking epicurean adventure in less-known parts and of a more modest nature, that of the 'Club-sans-Club' is indispensable. Let me acknowledge here and at once the debt that the gourmet, travelling in France, owes to these Guides. As also, to the three admirable volumes of M.J.-A. P. Cousin; on the whole, probably, though not so complete, the most trustworthy of them all. The well-known work of MM. Curnonsky and Rouff is a mine of information in matters bibulous and culinary, and is especially valuable in its receipts. It was published, however, over a period of years from 1921 to 1928, and, as is unavoidable, the character of many of the kitchens therein recorded has since changed. I have found it, on occasion, sadly at fault. But it is inevitable that any guide to good living, not published annually, should suffer from such defect: the course of true commerce running not always smoothly, and cooks, like other folk, being not immortal. Even within the space of two years, I myself have had to record the vanishing of two altars to the Hungry Traveller: the good Marius of Castellane having since died and the Hôtel Terminus, at Mâcon (once fit to vie with Bourg) having passed into unworthy hands.

The Annual, on the other hand, suffers from the very nature of its compilation. The ground it has to cover is so large, that it can but rely for its evidence upon a host of witnesses. No man of taste can have eaten everywhere and no man of moderation can enjoy more than two meals a day. In the record that follows hereafter of gastronomic itineraries, but a little over a hundred places are spoken of – or at least spoken well of – but they are one and all inns familiar to me. In no case do I praise where I have not eaten.

But to eat and drink is not all. However hungry may be the Hungry Traveller – however thirsty, the Thirsty – however delicately the Epicure may be tempted – if all these good things are ignobly offered, one may well leave such an hostelry to look after itself, and seek a welcome in plainer places. For I needs must regard the reader as also a Gentle Traveller, and to a man who is by nature Gentle, ill manners mortify the palate. So for this matter, not a few inns, which can boast a cellar – and even a cook – have here escaped my memory or, if remembered, have only been so remembered, in a cautionary spirit.

In considering the number of agreeable and comfortable houses of entertainment familiar to me throughout France, it has seemed to me most useful to the Traveller to group them in the form of specific itineraries. So that he who journeys by the compass may choose, as the mood takes him, to stop at such and such a place by the way or make a divagation from his straighter way at not too great a cost to his time or purse. This travel is also regarded as being undertaken by motor car – or, at least, by bicycle. France, as a whole, is a large country to walk in and the National Route is not built for the pedestrian. The passenger by train is necessarily limited to stations and junctions; and some of the best food in France takes days to get at by locomotive. The traveller by motor coach need not be considered. He is daily fed and watered at the whim of a Limited Liability Company – and such houses as his directors decide he can descend at, he can keep exclusively to himself. I shall not intrude – or urge the Hungry Traveller to intrude – into these symposia.

No man of sense would wish to dogmatise in matters of taste. It is a wise joint that knows its own gravy as it is a wise wine that knows its own grape. Accident and occasion govern all things. The adage has it that hunger is the best sauce, and the most succulent dishes and the choicest wines may be ruined by an east wind or a rainy day. The best gourmets among us are but creatures of circumstance. Unhappily, the art of eating and drinking is peculiarly susceptible to the devastating effect of snobbery. Criteria are imposed upon the *ipse dixit* of anonymities – no one knows how or why. To taste wine well is a recondite art; and, though many of us can taste wisely and correctly a comparative merit, very few indeed are able to pick out a Château – let alone a year; and *de gustibus non est disputandum* is as apposite to physical apperceptions as to mental judgments. Professor Bradley said that a critic can, after all, do no more than record his considered experience. When, in the following pages, I have stated a wine or a dish to be good or bad, it is understood that, with Professor Bradley, I am but citing a particular and remembered effect. Dives, himself, can do no more than this; Lazarus, no less.

Let us, for Heaven's sake, enjoy what we eat and drink, without too close a scrutiny in the matter. In these indulgences, a little knowledge is a dangerous thing – but I am not sure that more knowledge is not more so. It was Pasteur, I think, who said that he had spent fifty years in elucidating the secrets of nature, and it had left him with the faith of a peasant: and if he spent yet another fifty years in a similar activity, it would but leave him with the faith of a peasant's wife. *De nobis fabula.* Let us emulate wisely, as Epicureans, the faith of the peasant. At least, I am always grateful to sit at a peasant's table.

Of other matters in this book, a word or two will suffice. Three cities – Marseille, Lyon, and Bordeaux – I have treated apart from the itineraries. They are Capitals in Gastronomy – like Paris, of which I have omitted to speak. More Guides to Paris have been written than will ever be read and it were superfluous to supplement them.

A wine list has been included, as also a list of all the places gastronomically starred in Michelin (1931)[1] – with the omission of the larger towns (*e.g.* Nice, Strasbourg, Lyon, etc.). Some few places, which I have found to be unworthy of a star, I have also omitted. Places where Michelin's evidence is supplemented either by M. Cousin or myself (or both) are printed in heavy type.

The places are grouped in their departments, so as to enable the traveller to see, at a glance, the possibilities of the district around him.

[1] I have to thank this firm for their courtesy in allowing me to print this list.

FOREWORD

And lastly, to the Traveller who would turn resident, I have added a chapter upon life in France – with a special note upon Domestic Economy – such gloomy data as the French Income and other taxes being decently tabulated in the obscurity of an Appendix.

If in these desultory pages I have tickled the palate of the Hungry Traveller: enabled the Ingenious Traveller to comprehend more fully the variety of the French table and the fineness of the French mind and helped the Careful Traveller to balance a French Budget, the long labour and minute research which this *opusculum* has entailed will be fully repaid.

At the last and least, I write but for the Gentle and the Modest; and if, in any way, my direction has failed to fill the hungry with good things, I shall not feel broken-hearted, if, in the words of the Psalmist, it has sent the Rich empty away.

DIANO CASTELLO,
1931.

FIRST PART
GASTROGRAPHY

FIRST JOURNEY – DOWN

CHAPTER ONE

CHANNEL PORTS

There are four gateways into France open to the traveller from England in the course of common travel. They are Calais, Boulogne, Dieppe and Havre. Of the last-named I know less than nothing. I only once landed there – in charge of a miscellany of mules, horses, and lorries – and my gastronomic enterprise was then confined to bully beef and Maconochie. Dieppe, it is true, I know a little better; a little, but not much. I have been there a few times, but none within the last five years. Despite the fact that this town has given the name to one of the most delightful methods of cooking a sole, I do not remember to have eaten at all well there. I can recall a very bad meal at a very big hotel, whose name I shall forbear to advertise, as I presume it spends all its money in advertisement. It certainly spends little on its kitchen. At an earlier date, I stayed and fed modestly at a smaller establishment, since sold up. I can recall a young cub of an English-

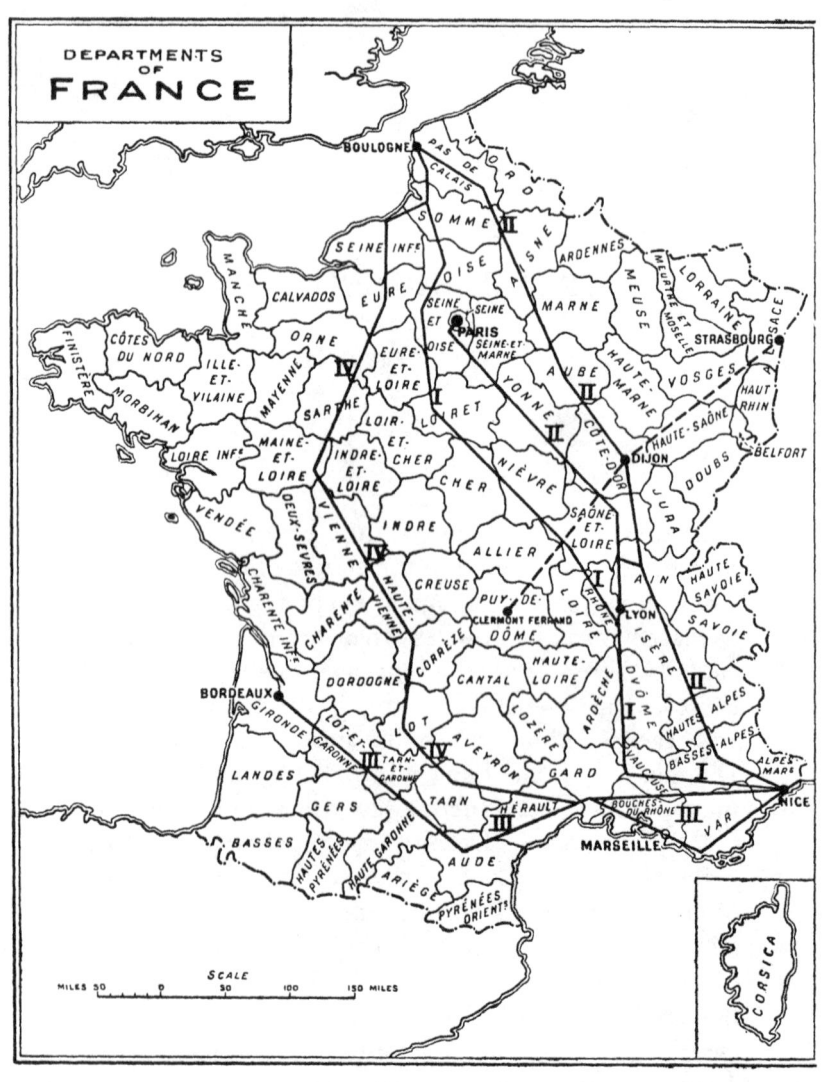

MAP SHOWING THE DEPARTMENTS OF FRANCE AND INDICATING (APPROXIMATELY) THE GASTRONOMIC ITINERARIES DETAILED IN THE TEXT

man who was uncivil to me in the Casino bar and a Mitteleuropan lady, of a commanding presence, who was a nuisance at the tables. Beyond this, my memory of Dieppe is vague. The place may well have improved since then; but I doubt it. It is too popular with summering Britons to be likely to offer much entertainment to the epicure. It may be observed that the town is unstarred (gastronomically) in Michelin (1931) and even the 'Club-sans-Club' is lukewarm about the place.

Calais I know better; but I have, personally, little to report to its credit. I have eaten there, better than elsewhere in the town, at the Station Buffet, in the Gare Maritime. But that is not saying much. I most earnestly recommend the fastidious to avoid the larger hotels in the town. I had as bad a dinner and at as extravagant a price in one of them as I can remember anywhere – apart from English seaside caravanserais. No doubt some miasma is blown from across the narrow straits to settle as a blight upon this once British port. Queen Mary may (or may not) have died with the name of Calais engraved upon her heart, but the gourmet might well do so with it engraved upon his liver. I do not say that you cannot find an inn worthy of Lucullus in Calais; I but report my own failure in the search; and I recommend the Traveller of Taste and Judgment to disembark at Boulogne.

Save for the through traveller to Paris, this substitution is of slight importance, unless train hours are inconvenient or the extra few minutes of sea passage is a consideration. Which reminds me that the meals provided on the 'Golden Arrow' – the last few times I used this convenience – were scarcely worthy of the epithet applied to the train, the country in which they were served, or the price one paid for them. To the motorist, however, this is, of course, of no moment. Let him, I repeat, unship himself and his shandrydan at Boulogne. The road from Calais is, in any case, a dreary one; and, in winter-time, sadly given to fogs. Calais, to be sure, is not unique in its possession of bad hotels. There are probably quite as many of these monstrosities in Boulogne as in Calais. Certainly one of the worst in the world is to be found in the former town and is too notorious to be named. Indeed, it was not until quite a recent date that I found in Boulogne a bed that pleased me at the price; a table fit to eat at, and that particular welcome which the Gentle Traveller has a right to expect.

I have the honour, herewith, to take off my hat to M. Paul Marmin, of the Brasserie Liégeoise.

The place is easy to find, being set in the very centre of the town, in that short street which runs up from the rue A. Thiers to the theatre. The traveller, however, who seeks it by car, should be warned as to one-way traffic streets, Boulogne having gone a little mad on the gyratory system. He should also be warned against falling in next door – namely, at the Excelsior: a restaurant of striking appearance without and but of poor entertainment within. And I might well take the occasion here to warn the seeker after good things against any external decorations imitative of olden times. 'Où sont les neiges d'antan?' asked the Vagabond Poet. 'Where are the snows of yesterday?' The right answer is, I think, that they are mostly melted by now. At any rate, hostelries nominated as such, timbered and painted and stuccoed to represent a past century, and labelled 'Auberge,' 'Rôtisserie,' and so forth, are, with a few brilliant exceptions, to be avoided. They are seldom better (and often worse) than 'Ye Olde Inne' swindle of the English country-side.

But the Brasserie Liégeoise is of a different order altogether. It is neither luxurious nor startling. It is not given to steels, mirrors and modern decoration. The restaurant is placed at one side of the café or brasserie, and partly screened off from it by a row of high-backed settees. The tables down one wall are, however, divided off by wooden partitions, much in the manner of some of the city eating-houses: a practical aid to privacy, not commonly met with in France. But there is nothing of what the French call 'chichis' about the house. The wood panels are as old as the house, but no older; nor is the guest shown the grease spot that the local celebrity made (or, more probably, did not make) with his head against it. It has the best of all recommendations to good food at a modest price, namely, the custom of the quarter. It is apt to be full at lunch-time; and, if one is late, one may have to wait for a table. In the evening, however, there is no such press. Also (a sure sign of merit) few English are to be met with there; although I did once lunch in front of a retired colonel, eating a lobster. He certainly was no less than this, for no one could have carried so rosy a face and such snowy moustaches without being alike a colonel and in retreat. But he ate his lobster so cleanly and cleverly and with such evident delight that I did not grudge him his discovery.

I can especially recommend there the moules

LE CHICHIS

marinières to such as enjoy the ubiquitous mussel. M. Marmin's mussels may, moreover, be depended upon: a point to bear in mind. I have met with mussels more dangerous than a Mills bomb. Also, *à propos* of mussels, his sole dieppoise is delicious. I do not remember ever having eaten a better dieppoise elsewhere. His specialities are his sole liégeoise and his homard à l'armoricaine; his terrine maison, the which I can especially praise: his goulash, his choucroute and his stuffed poulet. But the dish I best remember having eaten at the Liégeoise was a chicken, *cocotte*, with small onions, mushrooms and other vegetables. I think I once tasted as good a one at Fouquet's (upstairs) in Paris: but not a better. It must have had some special virtue in it, for I crossed the next day in one of the worst gales of the year without the slightest of qualms.

As to wine, I recommend the Burgundy. M. Marmin has some excellent Chablis at a sensible figure, and the more expensive wines are worth the price.

As to fine, take the Dennis Mounier, '65.

One can also sleep under the same roof as that under which one dines: a consideration if the weather be inclement or one's legs unsteady. The rooms are clean and comfortable; and one can even reserve to oneself a private bathroom. The coffee (chocolate) and rolls in the morning are as good as might be expected in regard to the dinner overnight.

Visitors staying in the house should not fail to make themselves acquainted with Madame's cat. This is an engaging animal that swings by its legs, with remarkable velocity, around a revolving hat-stand. It is an entertaining exhibition; but not one to be recommended to the diner who has taken a fine or two over the stipulated eight. He may be led to ascribe the phenomenon to his state of health. Lastly, and by no means least, the service, chez Marmin, is rewarded strictly upon a ten per cent. basis and is willingly and meticulously given. Experienced travellers will agree with me that to find so happy a combination is uncommon and deserves to be particularly remembered. I should add that there are two chasseurs of extreme minuteness and quite amazing efficiency, who perform varied duties, from posting letters and running out for cigars, to getting you telephone numbers and manœuvring luggage several sizes too large for them, who expect (and receive) honoraria in accordance with their size. I have come across many competent chasseurs in my time, but never any who contain so great a sagacity in so small a frame as these of the Brasserie Liégeoise. Also, you can, here (if you wish to) consult the Bottin.

Of other places of entertainment in Boulogne-sur-Mer, I wish I were able to say something worth the saying. And especially of Mony's, opposite the Brasserie. For during the years of war, Mony's was to many of us a Lucullian temple. What has happened there I do not know. Whether the original Mony of those days made so much money out of the English Army – let it be admitted, worthily and cheerfully spent – that he has long since retired with a competence, or perhaps something more: or whether so good an innkeeper has gone to wherever good innkeepers may be supposed to go upon the totting up of their last earthly addition, I cannot tell. All I know is that the Mony's of to-day is not at all as was the Mony's of yesterday.

Well, well – who knows? Perhaps we were hungrier then?

CHAPTER TWO

BEAUVAIS

It has always seemed to me no small compliment to the English that the main road from Paris to Calais, and so to London, should be numbered as the first of the National Routes. Perhaps the Corsican Adventurer, with his eye on England, gave it this priority. I do not know if our own authorities have similarly numbered the Dover Road as a compliment to France. If not, it is a question they might consider; but it is true that it is a long way back to the fifth Henry. However this may be, N.1 is a good road to travel upon: its surface is excellent, as indeed, is the case with most routes nationales. An exception I can recall is N.60, between Joinville and Troyes, which in '29 was certainly in a scandalous state. It may, of course, be repaired by now. Moreover, N.1 presents to the traveller the first lap of his journey south and impression is fresh to the mind. I have myself always especially enjoyed the morning's run from Boulogne. The first village of any size to be passed through is Samer. I have never stopped there, and all that I remember of it is the greasiness of its cobblestones. Less than an hour's run brings you to Montreuil, chiefly remarkable for having put up with the General Staff of the British Army for nearly four years. The ramparts are delightful: the Staff were happily unable to spoil those, but they so successfully spoiled the townsfolk that I recommend no one to stop within the town for refreshment – even if it be only of the liquid order. I have twice stopped there for an apéro', but in each case it was so insolently served and of so poor a quality that I have determined not to repeat the experiment. I remember during my brief stay in the town in '18 that the Hôtel de France was well able to cook a poulet, but the experiences noted above have not tempted me to discover if they still can. It is a pity, for Montreuil-upon-the-Sea (which incidentally it is not) is a picturesque little town and there are few better placed in France.

One can turn from here sharply to the right and reach Le Touquet and Paris Plage in some eighteen kilometres. In the summer-time, one may play games there and gamble and even bathe in the sea if one does not mind paddling for a couple of miles to get to it. Lots of people, I believe, go there (I have even been there myself – but not to eat), so I shall assume these places are sufficiently known to my fellow-countrymen and continue southward on the National Road. Less than half an hour upon this road brings us to Napont. A small village, where there is not much entertainment and less to look at: although I did once stop there to eat at the local estaminet (which is also the post office) and was comfortably, if rudely, fed with vegetable soup, an omelette, a stew and cheese. At least, I escaped having to dine at 'G.H.Q.' – I was journeying northwards at the time – moreover I felt called upon to halt here, partly for old associations' sake in war-time, but, more particularly, because it was here, the Informed Traveller will remember, that the Prince of all Travellers, and the Grand Master of the written word encountered the Franconian gentleman and his deceased donkey. Even La Fleur was moved in the matter; and I strictly enjoin the Sentimental Traveller to descend at the post office for a Pernod or Picon or whatever may please him, and duly drop a tear to the memory of poor Yorick and the dead ass.

Continuing along the Abbeville road one passes through the clean little village of Nouvion, with a correspondingly clean estaminet, where a meal of the humbler sort can be eaten. To the left lies the Forest of Crécy, with Crécy town upon the further side of it, to which I retired, with the remnants of the Fifth Army, in March of '18. It has always seemed to me a little cruel to have sent us there – under the circumstances – just 562 years too late – but perhaps General Headquarters had allowed their ironic humour the upper hand for the moment. I remember having discovered there, at that time, in the shop of a little old woman, a number of bottles of red Graves – a Pape Clément of '07, if my memory serves me aright – which I bought for the mess at a few francs a bottle. There is, however, none there now.

Of Abbeville I cannot speak with any knowledge. It is a town that I have no particular care for, although I found it agreeable enough when in retreat from the forward areas. The Tête de Bœuf used to be the best hotel. I must have eaten there a number of times, but all that I can remember of it now is an Australian captain who expectorated throughout dinner with great skill and persistence across his table on to the parquet floor. I have not dined in Abbeville since.

The next place of any size is Poix. I have never fed there myself, though I believe the Hôtel de Paris is not so bad inside as it looks from without. Of Grandvilliers, another 14 kilometres further on, I can speak with certainty; as well as praise with honesty. Indeed, I do this with a particular pleasure, since this little town is wholly unmentioned in any guide to gastronomy to which I have had access. The Hôtel de l'Angleterre is the house to choose. The set meal is excellent: I especially remember the vol-au-vent; and the place altogether is clean and comfortable. It is a convenient distance from Boulogne – 136 kilometres, a run of two and a half to three hours – and the traveller who is not in a hurry may well lunch there. Better there than at Marseille, another fifteen minutes further on. No, I do not mean that of the Bouches-du-Rhône; not being Mr. Harry Tate I do not do nine hundred kilometres in a quarter of an hour. I speak of Marseille-en-Beauvaisis.

There is an Auberge du Vieux Temps in this village. The name, to begin with, is suspicious; and the outside, of the worst sort of imitation oldness, calculated to catch the eye of the Foolish Traveller, is more so. I have never actually eaten therein. But I have been inside, which was quite enough. The place – it was already close on midday – was dirty and evil-smelling and, even at that hour, still being washed out. A slattern retailed to me a bill of fare of the quelconque variety, and while she disappeared into the kitchen, in the hope, I fancy, of finding something more appetising to suggest, I slipt out and on to Grandvilliers. In its 1931 edition, the 'Club-sans-Club' specifically recommends avoidance of this house.

From Marseille-en-Beauvaisis is only 19 kilometres to Beauvais. There are two things there that are almost unsurpassed anywhere else in France – the cathedral and the eating-house of the Châteaubriand.

This restaurant, small though it is, I would place among the first dozen in France (outside of Lyon and Paris) in respect both to the excellence of its cooking and the value of its cellar. It is easy to find, being situated just off the square of the town and on the main road in from the north. The gourmet's car may be conveniently parked immediately outside by backing it into the pavement; due care being taken not to knock over the oyster and other stalls, with which the front of the house is buttressed. These stalls, indeed, are complementary to the restaurant, providing a variety of shell-fish, from the larger oyster like the marenne to minute delicacies such as the winkle. Indeed, the Châteaubriand at Beauvais is the only place where I have ever eaten the humble winkle (so dear to the heart of the Cockney) never having been to Margate. The verisimilitude to this plebeian luxury is made complete by the provision of pins, neatly set in paper, but I must admit that I came to the opinion that the winkle is considerably overrated. One may, however, eat something else besides winkles at the Châteaubriand. I recommend the hors-d'œuvres to begin with (which include the pin and winkle), and as good a pâté maison as I have ever tasted: also the eels are admirable. But the feature of the Châteaubriand is the Côte de Veau bellovaque. This is a speciality of the district and is a veal chop, of an especial fatness, cooked, with mushrooms, in wine and cream. I can find no receipt for this dish and having omitted to ask the cook the exact method of its preparation, can only go by guesswork. However it is made, it is delicious eating: but it is a rich affair and one should be circumspect as to what one eats before and after. I well remember once, after a modest little meal there, of foie gras, fried eels, 'Bellovaque' and brie, washed down with Burgundy and old Armagnac, being somewhat indisposed afterwards; but the true epicure will be wiser than I was on that occasion. I may add that the cellar of the Châteaubriand is quite remarkable: I have drunk '87 Bonne Marres there and nowhere else. It conserves Burgundies both of a quality and at a price rare to find anywhere to-day. The Armagnac is also to be noticed, but I do not stand sponsor for the advertised Cocktail à la Maison: a concession, I presume, to the Anglo-American invasion. The Traveller of Taste and Discretion – or indeed anybody with a normally constituted stomach – is better without it. Yes: it is true that I once tried it: perhaps, for everything in this world is (I suppose) teleological, to be able to record my penitence in print.

    I would like to say something (after so much intestinal talk) of the – at least, to my mind – greatest Gothic cathedral in the world – but it is not, as far as these notes are concerned, in my vitrine. I urge even the Hungry Traveller to go and look at it – inside and out. But I suggest he does it before his visit to the Châteaubriand, rather than after: the effort of throwing back the head and gazing up into so high a heaven being distressful as a postprandial pose. You will find all about Beauvais Cathedral in Baedeker, Ruskin and others; but go and see it: for Heaven's sake go and see it when you are sober — dead sober. It should (if you have the soul of a louse, it will) make you drunk. I have only slept once at Beauvais — at the France et Angleterre. There may be a better hotel in the town: I trust there is. At the France and England — a name of ill-omen in most cases — I both dined and slept. The former was certainly a mistake, but I was in a pioneer mood and anxious to break fresh ground. I do not propose to break the same ground again. My room, I admit, was comfortable enough; although a party of English university students (mixed) with their guide, held a general purposes committee in the courtyard beneath my window until a late hour, finding (I presume) my host's wine more palatable than I did. Perhaps, my malaise was due to them. Patrons should always do well to remember, with Yorick, that Englishmen do not travel to meet other Englishmen. At any rate, however xenophobe they may be, they have no wish to be reminded of what America so elegantly calls 'sophomores' at one o'clock in the morning.

CHAPTER THREE

WITHIN THE ISLAND OF FRANCE

The traveller, while still at Beauvais, will already have entered the old province, so quaintly named the Île de France, of which the capital is Paris. I am not, in this book, presuming that my traveller is going into Paris. Should he wish to do that – and also feel hungry there – I advise him to purchase M. Cousin's Guide – Vol. I – which details 321 restaurants, citing their special dishes, their cellars and the character of their clientèle, as well as 34 resorts, not unhappily designated as 'Houses of Champagne' – to be visited, specifically, 'after midnight.' Bearing in mind the caveat as to change – and no town in the world changes so swiftly as 'Paname' – his book is the best on the gastronomy, and on what the French untranslatably call the *ambiance* of Paris that I know. I will assume rather that my traveller is essentially a Provincial Traveller and eager to reach the south without too great a delay or distraction.

To such an one the most convenient route is to leave Paris on the left, journeying south. In my next itinerary, I will detail a road from south to north to the east of Paris, but such is better done by N.37, viâ Arras and Soissons. Having travelled upon N.1 as far as Beauvais it is a needless (and confusing) détour to pass eastward viâ Meaux, unless one has a specific reason for so doing.

The traveller wishing to go direct to Paris continues, of course, by the first National Route, entering in at the Porte de la Chapelle.

The south-bound traveller, moving west of Paris from Beauvais (to, say, Orleans) may pass conveniently either on the inner road through Pontoise, St.-Germain and Versailles or on the outer, through Mantes and Chartres. To take the inner road first, one follows the National Route as far as Allone (of tragic memory), there taking a sharp turn to the right into G.C.135. Unlike most roads in this category of 'Grandes Communications' – a class to be looked upon, in general, by the careful driver, with suspicion – this particular one is in good condition. It passes one of the dreariest towns in the province (Meru – they make mother-of-pearl there!) to Pontoise, on (as one would imagine) the Oise. One must take care here to get on to N.184, and cross the Seine at Conflans. Otherwise, one runs on into suburban Paris on N.14, or N. 192, and having been once caught up in the welter of side streets and the maelstrom of trams and buses, taximeter cabriolets and (towards dusk) the outgoing motor traffic of the daily breader, one will be lucky if one finds St.-Germain with a whole mudguard. I once made this mistake myself – and having comfortably lost myself in the maze of Asnière, Courbevoie and Puteaux, took about two hours to get to St.-Germain-en-Laye, a bare 15 kilometres away. If you don't believe me, get a large-scale map and see what it looks like: or try it for yourself, but don't blame me afterwards. . . .

Avoiding, however, such disasters, and crossing the river safely at Conflans, a quarter of an hour brings you to St.-Germain – a pleasantly situated town, of historical association, an adjacent forest, high rents, and a spacious hotel, with proportionately exorbitant charges. I have never stayed, save once, in the place, except with friends. I fancy the latter is the better way to stay there, if possible. At any rate, I do not recommend the hotel, at which I put up on that solitary occasion. It has a view, I admit. But unless you wish to play the part of a modern Ste. Geneviève and overlook a sleeping Paris at a very special price, I would not suggest staying the night there. You may walk upon the terrace and drink a cocktail for the price that such places charge: the which, I feel sure, is quite enough for both exercises.

From St.-Germain-en-Laye to Versailles is 13 kilometres, still along N.184. This latter town can boast one of the ugliest palaces and some of the most extortionate hotels in all France. I remember in one of these latter having quite a modest meal, à la carte, which cost me nearly two hundred francs: a charge of ten francs being made for butter. It is true that, in return for this extravagance you could dine in a room as big as a railway station, in a select company wholly Anglo-American, and that you were not required – indeed, you were not allowed – to speak French. I did not, however, consider these amenities worth the money and I have not been there since.

But one can still eat well – very well – in Versailles; at a modest cost and in an atmosphere more *gemüthlich* than is to be found in these palaces; and I advise the Humble Traveller to search out the Restaurant Pilloud – it is no longer of Pilloud, but the name remains up over the house – in the rue André Chenier, behind the market.

One must not be put off by the humbleness of the place. Having, as the French have it, 'passed the zinc'; or, in other words, the café-bar outside, one enters into the tiny restaurant behind. Its smallness is in comparison to its worth and you will scarcely find better cooking around Paris at the price. I ate one of the best civets there I have eaten anywhere: and the Pouilly is good and cheap. I have never stayed a night in Versailles and I do not imagine the Traveller of Taste and Circumspection will wish to do so either. If, however, he wishes to visit Paris for a day or two he may park his car there. To the owner-driver, at least, a car in Paris is apt to be a white elephant: taxis being as numerous and excellent as they are cheap; although driving is easier in Paris than in London and the parking facilities infinitely more so. And in this matter I can very strongly recommend the Garage des Chantiers – in rue des Chantiers. I myself have left my car there a great number of times and it happily combines two qualities, rare in garages, competence and honesty. The daily charge is, or was, ten francs; compared to twenty-five francs demanded by the garages of the central arrondissements. Sixty francs can thus, for example, be saved in four days, to balance against the taxi account. I might add, what is not commonly known to the foreigner, a word as to taxis outside Paris. If one wishes to taxi into Paris (from Versailles, for instance) take a Versailles taxi to the Porte St.-Cloud and change there, inside the gate, into a Paris taxi. As the basic rate of the latter is less than that of the former and you do not have to pay a return fare within the walls of Paris, your journey from Versailles to (say) the Place de l'Opéra will cost you about forty-five francs if you change taxis, compared to about eighty if you do not. But to leave Paris out of the question and to keep to the road. If one wishes to run through Versailles, one can conveniently lunch, some minutes later, at the little town so oddly called Robinson. Of the origin of this, or who the original Robinson was or why he planted the great tree that dominates the place, I fear I am ignorant. But it is a quaint spot well worth a visit. One turns off N.186 to the left — the first road after passing the cross-roads at Petit Clamart. About a mile along this side road one finds the Restaurant of the True Tree of Robinson on one's right. The food there is excellent and the view superb — especially if you climb the tree. But do not go there on a Sunday: it is then apt to be a bear-garden. Continuing along the circular road numbered 186 one can either turn off to the right into N.20 at the Croix de Berny, making for Orléans through Étampes, or one can go on to the Belle Épine and so into N.7, the great road south out of the Porte d'Italie, and on to Fontainebleau and Sens. I shall treat of this road in a separate itinerary later. The student of cartology, by the way, will discover an apparent short-cut from Versailles, on G.C.68, through Orsay, cutting into N.7, by Corbeil. I do not advise it: it is not as short as it looks on the map. If, however, one decides to skirt Paris on the outer road, it is best to begin this divagation from Beauvais itself, taking N.181 to Gisors and thence through Magny to Mantes. Of Gisors I know nothing, having but passed through it, but I can heartily recommend the Hungry Traveller to stop at Mantes. It is only some 70 kilometres from Beauvais and if one is in no hurry one may well take the occasion to lunch there at the Grand Cerf. The other house of the town – the Hostelry of the Isle of the Ladies – the which you come upon first, is pleasantly situated on the north bank of the river, within an extensive park. This house has a history and has (or had) a reputation. I stopped to look at the place, but was not agreeably impressed by it (I may well be mistaken); and I went on to the Grand Cerf. Of this hotel I speak, at least, both from experience and with approval. It has a competent chef, the bill of fare is varied and well chosen, and there is a set meal at a reasonable figure. The style of the house is pleasant. There is a garden at the back and the courtyard in front can accommodate your own car, as well as several others – which it commonly does.

Should one wish to make a longer morning's run from Beauvais, one may pass through to Houdan on N.183, turning off the national road some 10 kilometres past the latter place into G.C.61 as far as

St.-Léger and thence into G.C.138, which brings one to Rambouillet unless one loses one's way in the process – as I did (quite successfully) the first time I tried this cross-country cut. Rambouillet is only 124 kilometres from Beauvais, but since the latter part of the route is (as I have pointed out above) somewhat intricate, a good three hours should be allowed for the run.

At Rambouillet, one must on no account fail to lunch – or, dine and sleep, as the case may be – at the Hostellerie de la Garenne. This hostelry is one of those exceptions that prove the rule in general as to houses painted and plastered to represent the past and saddled with an antique appellation. Its name alone is suspicious and its appearance more so. It is garish and grandiloquent to a degree and placed, unhandily, on the outskirts of the town and away from the main road. But do not be discouraged by all this. Its welcome within is in inverse ratio to its appearance without, and I have eaten there not only one of the best dinners, but also one of the best served dinners, I can recall over a period of years. There is there an elderly maître-d'hôtel of a type uncommon in France, being not only in face and figure, but also in manners and address, the perfect type of the old family butler. I feel sure he must have been something of the sort, before he descended into the hurly-burly of hotel life. One also finds there a bedroom with private bathroom, of the first comfort, and at a most reasonable price; and the welcome of the house as a whole is as cordial as its kitchen is comforting. But a word of warning should be added. The middle of the week is the best time to enjoy this hospitality. Rambouillet is too near Paris, and the Hostellerie de la Garenne too well known to Parisians for it to be anything but overcrowded of a week-end – especially in summer time.

Of other eating-houses in Rambouillet, I have lunched at the Relais du Château, which Michelin decorates (to my mind, undeservedly) with three stars. At any rate, I advise the Traveller of Taste to take the trouble to seek out the Garenne. I do not think he will be disappointed.

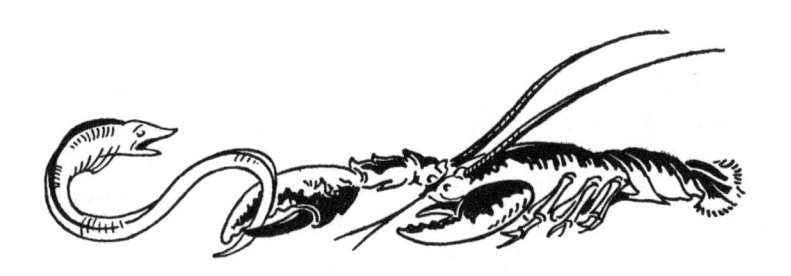

CHAPTER FOUR

THROUGH THE ORLÉANAIS

The traveller moving southward through the Orléanais has a variety of routes open to him. He may continue directly on N.154 to Chartres; presuming he did not branch off eastward into Rambouillet. At Chartres he may dine and sleep, expensively, as befits a cathedral town, whose monument attracts so many sightseers from all over the world every year. I recommend, therefore, the traveller who regards throwing money into the rapacious maw of the hotel-keeper as unnecessary, and civil treatment an essential, to confine his activities at Chartres more particularly to the cathedral. It is better than the hotels – and cheaper.

From Chartres to Orléans is a short run of 71 kilometres. At Orléans there is also a cathedral. Its specialities are quince cakes, chicken pâtés, vinegar and Joan of Arc. The last, in one form or another, is inescapable; and my own feelings toward Orléans are not unsimilar to those which I cherish for Chartres.

The traveller anxious to escape from the historic and the monumental into a less fervid atmosphere may do well to push on to the little town of Châteauneuf-sur-Loire, another 25 kilometres upstream.

One can eat and drink peculiarly well in this quiet and comfortable place. But I warn the Hungry Traveller to eschew the venerable Feuillaubois. That M. Feuillaubois was chef to the Prince Borghese in 1875 I do not doubt – but it is a devilish long time ago – and this doyen of French cooking must be well on in his eighties. I learnt that he still kept a heavy hand on affairs, which might well account for failure. A pity, in an old house, that might well have conserved its quality under other management.

But I can advise the epicure, with all confidence, to stop at the other hotel in the village, the Parc: a house, situated just outside the château gates. This clean and excellent little hotel deserves, to my mind, to be specially recommended to the travelling public. The welcome is all that such should be; Madame herself does the cooking, and very good indeed it is. I can remember, especially, a pike cooked in butter, with chives and grated biscuit. I found the place – being a little out of love with the House of Feuillaubois – by asking at the local pharmacy where one could feed best in the place. This, by the way, is a procedure I recommend to every traveller abroad – or in England as far as that goes. In France such inquiry is always to the good. Not necessarily at a shop, but of anyone in the street; reasonable care being taken to select a man (not a woman), and one, if possible, between forty and fifty, slightly given to corpulence. Do not overdo this, or the man may be on a diet of charcoal and Vichy water, and be unable to advise you, save from hearsay. One can also conveniently make such inquiries at the café where one takes an apéritif; but be sure first that the café does not also serve meals. As to kinds of people to ask such questions of, I can heartily recommend a policeman – of the right sort. But one should use judgment in the matter and not question him, gastronomically, when he is trying to eliminate a traffic jam. Policemen's tempers are no longer than anybody else's. Of shopkeepers I do not recommend either butchers or grocers: they deal, perhaps, too much in eatables to know how to eat. I have generally found apothecaries and bank clerks knowledgeable; and the parish priest (if you can get hold of him) best of all. Inquiries of this sort may often coincide with the recommendations of guide-books and the like; but, as often, not. Change and mortality (as I have already pointed out) are so omnipresent in this world that the most meticulous of guidebooks are bound to be, in many cases, out of date almost as soon as printed. Ask, by all means. Ask everybody you can get to answer you. And when, in any particular town or village, Michelin and the 'Club-sans-Club,' Messrs. Cousin, Curnonsky and Rouff, the policeman, the local bank-manager, the apothecary, the curé – and myself, all agree that X is the house to dine at – certainly dine there. You will have probably found the best restaurant in the place.

It was not more than an hour's journey from Châteauneuf-sur-Loire that I met, as an explorer in gastronomy, my Waterloo. Perhaps had I eaten on the advice adumbrated above, and inquired of local pundits, I might have been spared a tiresome

IT IS NOT THE MOMENT TO MAKE GASTRONOMICAL INQUIRIES

journey, poor entertainment and an uncomfortable night. But thrilled by the echoes of a reputation that still seems to reverberate throughout the epicurean library — M. Curnonsky is almost lyrical about it — I went miles out of my path to discover Pithiviers. I discovered it — eventually; after leaving the main road (N.154) at Allaines — and losing myself a number of times in some of the ugliest and worst by-roads in all France.

This house of Laumonier, at Pithiviers, is stated to have been in the same family for several generations, but something certainly seems to be amiss with the present, or I arrived on a day when the members of the family that mattered were on holiday and Cousin Jane's sister's young man's aunt cooked the dinner. Moreover, the house smelt of stale pastry, from the pastry-shop without to the dining-room within, even filtering coyly into the bedrooms. It is all very well for M. Curnonsky to call it the 'Mecca of lark patties and the Metropolis of almond icing,' but the former scarcely tempted me, and the latter I heartily detest. I dined there — it was too late to go anywhere else — and ate a number of dishes, equally indifferently served. The one stray gleam, in an otherwise wholly gloomy evening, was a good bottle of Burgundy, for which I paid an appropriate price. After dinner, I went out into the town (such as it is) in the hope of finding a café of a quiet order, favourable to a ruined palate and jaded nerves. I only succeeded in falling into a buvette, noisy with a number of drunk cyclists, and at last went to bed in a dingy and ill-ventilated room, such as I hope not to encounter again. No: I fear I have no use for Pithiviers, in spite of its almost official réclame. M. Cousin, I gather, from his discreet silence, feels much the same way about it as I do.

If one has been lucky (or unlucky) enough to reach Pithiviers, one may well go on, viâ D.7 and D.11, until one strikes the national road at Ludon and thence to Montargis. The Southern Traveller will then turn to the right and along N.7 to Nogent-sur-Vernisson, some 17 kilometres further south. Here, for his stomach's sake, I adjure him to stop. Of the Hotel of the Puy-de-Dôme at this Nogent, I find it hard to speak without hyperbole. If there is one house of call in all France where the Humble, the Gentle, the Delicate, the Clean, the Comfort-loving and the Hungry Traveller can one and all be satisfied, it is at the house of M. Jean Labasse at Nogent. It is, of necessity, a small and humble house in as proportionately small and unimportant a village. If the Proud Traveller is ill-affected by these externals – so much the better. There is less chance of him making himself a nuisance in a place which every true epicure should regard with affection and esteem. Indeed, I sincerely trust that all Britons with large banking-accounts, luxury cars, loud voices and bad manners will find even the look of the place so little to their taste that they will push on to Nevers, where they will find a hotel quite as large as their ideas, complete with uniformed porters, private baths, American bars and all the comforts that modern civilisation can provide for the weary (and wealthy) traveller. But for him of a fine appetitie and an equal mind there are few inns to be found to suit him better than the Puy-de-Dôme.

The House itself is long, low and whitewashed, of only two stories, with a large yard and outhouses behind. It is built very much upon the plan of — indeed, it probably originally was — a farm-house of the district. It is as spotlessly clean inside as it is out. One goes through the small café to be most cordially welcomed by M. Labasse. Madame Labasse herself does the cooking and is the proud possessor of the *Golden Book* of the 'Club-sans-Club,' a distinction accorded to the very few, and only after extended proof of great culinary merit. That Madame Labasse fully deserves this honour — and the many known signatures in the *Golden Book* itself are witnesses thereof — one has only to eat there oneself to see. There are three set menus, at most modest prices, and the traveller can thus conveniently consider both his purse and his digestion. I fear I was greedy enough to choose the longest one; but I did not regret it, either then or afterward. I must especially mention the kidneys cooked in red wine and the purée of potatoes with egg and butter — a dish not quite so easy as it sounds. I accompanied the meal with a bottle of Aloxe-Corton of '19, of real distinction. But Madame Labasse can not only cook; she has also a wonderful way with animals. Talk of dogs with her, and she will be delighted. She will show you those she has, and especially an intelligent terrier which runs up a steep ladder after rats in a loft. I am too fond of dogs to enjoy canine performances as a rule, but this is of another order; and to see the animal coming down the ladder, with all the care and pomposity of an elderly clubman coming downstairs is as entertaining an exhibition as you could wish to see anywhere. I need scarcely add that the sleeping accommodation is in accord with everything else in this agreeable little house.

Should the traveller wish to pass from Orléans to Nevers by the westerly loop, through Vierzon and Bourges rather than through Gien and Cosne, he will cut across the old province of the Berry. He will take the opportunity, no doubt, to visit the cathedral of Bourges, one of the finest piles in France, and see some of the most beautiful stained glass in the world. As to the comforting of the body, apart from the comforting of the soul, I have found Bourges not unlike other cathedral cities. Great monuments seem to debauch the minds of innkeepers. I found my hotel there uncomfortable, its service negligent and its charges high. I have also dined at what is supposed to be the best restaurant in the town – that of the Escargot d'Or. Its prices are in inverse ratio to its merits – the former being as high as the latter are low. I remember trying to eat there a civet de lièvre, which seemed to contain the abatis of almost every animal except a hare. I suggested to the maître d'hôtel that it must contain at least thirty-six livers. But my irony was ill received: the fellow but assured me that that was quite impossible, as what hare could have thirty-six livers? This one had, anyhow; and I earnestly recommend any traveller, with a single and delicate one, to avoid the Golden Snail.

CHAPTER FIVE

THE NIVERNAIS AND LOWER BURGUNDY

If the traveller, however, prefers to follow, from Orléans, the valley of the Loire, he will come into N.7 at Briare. If he has stayed the night at Châteauneuf-sur-Loire, it is a short and pleasant morning's run from there to Pouilly-sur-Loire. In this agreeable little town, one may lunch remarkably well at the unpretending, but excellent, little Hôtel de l'Espérance. It is a peculiarly happy name for it, for the hope of the gourmet is adequately fulfilled. I had a modest, but extremely good meal there, of hors-d'œuvre, œufs Bercy, carré de Porc, with white beans, pâté de lièvre and salad, cheese and fruit, being the set meal for the day; and drank some of the Pouilly wine (not to be mistaken for the Burgundy of the same name of the Mâconnais) the which is neither so good as it is advertised to be nor as bad as it is sometimes supposed. I drank there a bottle of this wine – Blanc Fumé – Côtes du Nues – which was by no means unpleasant. The better-known house in Pouilly – on the other side of the street from the Espérance – was established (I understand) by the Company of the Wines of the Loire to bring their peculiar vintages to the notice of the public. It may be all that it is made out to be, but, having looked inside the place, I preferred to seek humbler entertainment elsewhere.

If one should wish to increase the morning's run by another quarter of an hour or so, one may well stop at la Charité-sur-Loire, a charming old town, finely situated on the bank of the river. Of the Hôtel de la Poste et du Grand Monarque there, I have no personal knowledge, but it looks an agreeable and unspoilt house from without and probably is such within. I myself dined and stayed the night at a smaller inn up the main road on the north side of the town: namely the Hôtel Terminus. It is a modest place, but with an excellent table, being honourably mentioned by the Union of Commercial Travellers. It is almost needless to add that if you follow in the footsteps of commercial gentlemen, you may be sure of finding the best cooking at the least cost.

From la Charité to Nevers is only a matter of 24 kilometres. One passes through Pougues-les-Eaux and one can take the waters there if one has a mind that way. I have never stopped there myself and so do not know if there is anything else to be got there besides the waters. Of Nevers, I fear also I have little of interest to report. I have dined there – at the principal hotel – and found it no better and no worse than its size and character had led me to expect.

If you should wish to visit Moulins, you can continue upon N.7, into the Bourbonnais, and from there, still

THE NIVERNAIS AND LOWER BURGUNDY 59

upon the Seventh National, through Lapalisse and Roanne into Lyon; or more directly south, on N.82, through Feurs and St.-Etienne. At Moulins, one is only 27 kilometres from Vichy, where more water may be drunk. Moulins, I have passed through, but never stopped at, and I am a kind of French Mr. Pickwick, being (possibly) the only person in France who has never stayed at Vichy. I have, however, drunk several tons of its bottled waters; and can recommend the nastiest as being the most effective.

Should one wish to cross into Burgundy and drop into the valley of the Saône to the north of Lyon, one can either pass directly from Nevers to Mâcon on N.79 (177 kilometres); or, from Moulins, branch into N.79 at Diou, on C.12, viâ Dompierre-sur-Barbre. This last is not to be recommended, if the road is still in the same state as it was last year. I struck it first when moving northwards in May last, having mistaken the main road to Nevers outside Diou; and I made the same blunder again in November. The road direction is here unusually bad and the first part of C.12 – or rather C.46, as it is as far as Dompierre – appearing to be the better and more direct route. I have come across some bad roads in France, but none so continuously abominable as this, where the unhappy driver may encounter at least 20 kilometres of almost contiguous pot-holes, reducing his speed, if he has any care for his car, to a walking pace. For at least six months last year no effort at repair had been made at all! It is, happily, rare now to find roads of any importance in France in such a state: but C.12 is a scandalous exception which deserves to be so recorded. Presuming the traveller to have left la Charité after lunch; and to have kept to N.79, avoiding Moulins, a matter of just 200 kilometres brings him to Mâcon. This road is a perfect one and he may well do the run in four hours; but should he wish to loiter he may conveniently stay the night at Charolles, thus reducing his journey by 54 kilometres. The Golden Lion, in this pleasant little town, is a small, but agreeable house to stop at. Its cooking is as sound as its welcome is sincere.

Should the south-bound traveller wish to delay his journey by making a raid into the Auvergne, he can very comfortably do so from Charolles. I have taken this road myself to Clermont-Ferrand, a city which I would urge the gastronomically adventurous to visit. The total distance from Charolles to Clermont is only 180 kilometres. This distance may be done in an afternoon, perhaps, in summer-time; but, in winter weather, the road is perilous – if not impassable. I attempted it at the end of February and was snowed up at nightfall on the Croix St.-Martin (3000 feet) and only reached Thiers that night by the aid of a yoke of oxen which pulled me over the col. In any case, I would advise the Hungry Traveller to stop for lunch at la Clayette. It is true that this little town is only 20 kilometres from Charolles, but one can, of course, spend the previous night further back than Charolles, so as to divide the day better. But la Clayette is not a place to be missed by the earnest epicure. I will not go so far as to say that it provides the best meal to be found in France – but I think I may justly go so far as to say that it serves the best meal to be found (or, rather, that I have found) in France for 20 francs or 3s. 3d.

THE NIVERNAIS AND LOWER BURGUNDY

The house, which entertains the traveller so comfortably at so modest a price, is the Hôtel Lauriot, opposite the railway station. Like almost every good house of this class, it is peculiarly affected by commercial travellers. Indeed, I am credibly informed – and I can well believe it – that no commercial has ever been known to omit la Clayette from his itinerary, no matter how unsuitable the goods he travelled in might be to this modest township of eighteen hundred souls in the Saône-et-Loire.

The lunch I ate there myself was as follows:

> Pâté foie-gras
> Salmon trout (meunière)
> Pommes au gratin
> Roast veal
> Salad
> Cheese

The list is, perhaps, not a particularly imposing one, but its excellence was beyond praise. To begin with, the pâté was real goose liver pâté. The salmon trout was as fine a one as I have ever eaten, and cooked to a turn. The pommes au gratin would have graced the tables of Point, de France or Caramello and the roast veal *was* roast veal. The salad was delightful and new to me, being of mâche (or doucette); the English thereof, being, I understand, corn-salad. The specialities of the house are quenelles de brochet à la crème, écrivisse, truite and vins du Beaujolais. I drank there, with my lunch, firstly some of their wine en carafe – a Beaujolais of an excellent character – and afterwards a Corton of '23. I can also recommend the Marc. la Clayette, by the way, is not only of gastronomic

COMMERCIAL GENTLEMEN KNOW WHERE TO DINE

THE NIVERNAIS AND LOWER BURGUNDY 63

interest. It boasts one of the most picturesque châteaux, complete with moat, that I have found apart from the notable and advertised examples. I might add that G.C.71, from Charolles to la Clayette is (or was) by no means a pleasure to drive over. But one must pay something – if only in tyre wear – for these unspoilt oases.

Thirty-nine kilometres from la Clayette brings one to Roanne, a town of some forty thousand inhabitants and small attraction. I lunched there once – at the Grand Hôtel et Gare – and though the food was not uneatable, the manners of the staff did not tempt me to repeat the experiment. A pity – for I imagine the house had, at one time, a reputation. Perhaps its proximity to Vichy renders it liable to be debauched by tourists.

The most direct road from Roanne to Thiers and Clermont-Ferrand is to follow N.81 as far as Villemontais, then by G.C.53 to St.-Just-en-Chevalet, but a better road is the National (N.81) viâ Cremaux and Jure. From St.-Just one continues on N.81 over the col, cutting into N.89 at Chabreloche – a pretty road in summer, but, as I have pointed out, not to be attempted with snow about. Seventy-six kilometres from Roanne brings one to Thiers. If the traveller wishes to stop here, he can be strongly recommended to stay at the sign of the Golden Eagle. It is a sound old-fashioned house, of the better sort, with an excellent kitchen and a welcome to match. It is true it sports an AA sign over its portals, but the English tripper does not seem, as yet, to have been ubiquitous enough to ruin the place. I ate a pleasant little dinner there – including some delightful egg cutlets – and drank afterwards a Cognac, by a house new to me, namely Emile Engrand – which I think deserves notice.

An hour's run from Thiers brings one to Clermont-Ferrand, chiefly notable for the Michelin tyre factory and precious stones of the amethyst variety. The Michelin Guide (perhaps out of an exaggerated sense of delicacy) denies its home town the honour of any gastronomic star. It fully deserves a stellar galaxy – for this busy town of over 100,000 inhabitants does not live entirely upon india-rubber, even in an economic sense. It conserves at least two restaurants of the first order – the Gastronome and the Brasserie de Strasbourg. Personally, I prefer the latter.

As to hotels, I can recommend the Grand Hôtel, in the Place Jaude: a thoroughly modernised house, at a moderate price for the comfort provided. Almost next door to it is the Brasserie. The last time I lunched there I ate as follows:

> Snails
> Tournedos with pommes frites
> Cêpes
> Salade
> Soufflet of pineapple with Kirsch

The last-named item was a veritable dream. Those who know how difficult it is to find a cook who can make a soufflet, will appreciate my enthusiasm in this matter. I drank, with this excellent meal, Pommard, of 1921, of the Hospice de Beaune; and afterwards, some of the best Armagnac I have found anywhere – a veritable '58. I should like to add that the service at the Brasserie is as prompt and courteous as its kitchen is good.

The motorist may be warned that Clermont-Ferrand is by no means an easy town to find one's way either in or out of: a careful study of the plan of the town is to be recommended. But to return to Charolles – to N.79 and the journey south. At Mâcon, all the world knows the Hotel of Europe and England. I have not myself been there since 1927, having deserted it for the Hôtel Terminus, now, alas, in unworthy hands. The former is one of the best-advertised houses of call for the Riviera traffic; its courtyard being filled with motor-cars as its dining-room is with guests. Its kitchen, its cellar and its charges are all of the first order.

Of other places in the town, of a more modest kind, I know only of the Restaurant Lamartine on the quay of that name. It is not, of course, the Hôtel de l'Europe, but you can get quite a sound meal there à la carte, at a moderate price. Personally, I have little love for Mâcon, as a town. I do not know if it is particularly red, but I have always found it, like Chalon on the same river, overcrowded with the sort of lout that is a staunch supporter of the left wing of the United Socialists.

Perhaps the sight of so many luxury cars outside the Hotel of Europe and England makes your Mâconnais feel like that?

CHAPTER SIX

THE LOWER RHÔNE

From Mâcon to Lyon is only 70 kilometres. It is an excellent road, and I have done the run in as many minutes. Of Lyon – the very hub of the gastronomic world and the *fons et origo* of French cooking – I shall say nothing in this itinerary, reserving a special chapter for it later. I will suppose the traveller to have passed through (or around) Lyon and to have reached Vienne, 28 kilometres further down the river. And it may not be out of place, here, to indicate to the traveller moving south from Nevers, an alternative route. The best way to accomplish this is to leave the National Route N.79 at Digoin, turning to the right into C.77 (later C.10 bis) as far as Roanne. Or if we suppose the traveller to have slept at Charolles he must take C.71 from that place and then by C.78 and C.10 bis into Roanne. From Roanne he must follow N.7 for 10 kilometres, then taking the right-hand road, namely, N.82, to Feurs. From Feurs he takes the National, N.89 as far as the tiny village of Duerne, branching here to the right into G.C.34, as far as Givors. This piece of road is remarkably lovely. One climbs to a height of over

THE LOWER RHÔNE

2000 feet and enjoys a magnificent panorama; and the road, though but a by-road, and naturally very twisted, is excellent as to surface. At Givors, one comes into the main road again (N.86), and one follows the western bank of the Rhône as far as Vienne, some dozen kilometres further down the river.

The whole of this journey from Charolles is about 170 kilometres. The winding nature of the road, of course, delays one; nor does the Observant Traveller wish to pass through beautiful country too quickly; but some four hours should suffice for the completion of this stage. Thus, if a moderately early start is made, one may arrive at Vienne comfortably for lunch. There is, also, all the reason in the world that the Epicure should do this.

Throughout all the length and breadth of France, and excepting the four capitals of Paris, Lyon, Marseille and Bordeaux there are, to my own particular knowledge and understanding, five restaurants that stand out above all others as Lucullian temples. One, I have already spoken of – the Châteaubriand at Beauvais. The second to be noticed in these travels is the Restaurant of the Pyramide at Vienne. The three others will be treated of in due course, as one comes to them. It is invidious to make comparisons, so (with the exception of one of the four, to whom homage will be paid later as, in my opinion, at least, the Grand Master Cook of the world), I will not attempt to give any order of precedence to these remaining three. Such can only be a matter of individual taste and accident. It remains but to repeat that, as far as I know, after this master, M. Point, of the Pyramide, M. de France of the Châteaubriand, an ex-chef of the King of Norway, and a certain M. Marchant – at a railway station – are to be regarded as his worthiest disciples.

It happens (perhaps fortunately) that the Restaurant of the Pyramide is not too easy to find. The motoring public may easily miss it. In the first place, it is outside the centre of the town and then down a small side street, not to be noticed unless you are looking for it. This is the short Boulevard of the Pyramide, which lies on the right-hand side of the main road south as you leave the town. Having passed around the 'Pyramide' – which is an obelisk – one finds oneself at the Restaurant, an unpretending house set in a garden, where one can conveniently leave one's car. M. Point has two set meals, at different prices. The last time I had the honour of lunching there I chose (I am afraid I always do; but then I am thoroughly greedy) the more elaborate and expensive one; and I happen to have conserved a note upon it. The menu was as follows:

> Pâté de foie gras
> Saucissons de Ménage
> Galantine de Volaille
> Gratin de Queues d'Écrevisses Nantua
> Pommes de Terre à la Mode dauphinoise
> Perdreaux rôtis sur Canapés
> Crème au Chocolat
> Crème fraîche de Bresse
> Fruits
> Pâtisserie

The price of such is (or was) 45 francs: considering the dishes and the perfection of the cooking, by no means an extravagant account.

The saucisson was a marvel in itself and the écrevisse tails, cooked in cream and white wine, a dream. Pommes dauphinoises is a delicate dish of potatoes, finely sliced and cooked in milk, butter and egg. A roast partridge is, of course, a roast partridge: at least, it should be. This one was. More than a century ago, Brillat Savarin delivered the aphorism: 'On devient cuisinier, mais on naît rôtisseur.' M. Point must, I feel sure, have been born and not made a cook, for he knows how to roast. I can only add that both the creams and the pastry of this perfect meal were of the same quality as their preceding dishes. I drank with this meal a Richebourg '19, at the very reasonable price of 50 francs the bottle. Should the traveller wish to sleep at Vienne, the Hôtel du Nord can be recommended. It also boasts an excellent table, at a modest price.

If one has the heart (or the strength), after lunching at the Pyramide, to go any further, one continues down the Seventh National, with the Rhône upon one's right hand. Fifty-five kilometres brings one to Tain, where the Hermitage comes from: a wine less known in England than it once was. I have never eaten at Tain, but the Hôtel Hermitage has, I believe, a deserved reputation. Of Valence, another 18 kilometres further on, I know more. It has the distinction of possessing one of the worst run, worst mannered and correspondingly highest priced hotels between Lyon and Avignon. Do not go there. Go rather to the Hôtel de l'Europe. This hotel has quite recently been renovated; and I have not stopped there since the transformation. I trust that the money spent on paint and plate glass, bars, bathrooms and the like to attract the Anglo-

Saxon, has not been deducted from the salary of the cook. For it had, when I knew it, a very fine table. A table of that particular kind, where the most select and successful commercial travellers gather together to discuss business, to tell stories and to peck a morsel of food. That was four years ago; it might well have changed by now.

After leaving Valence – which boasts, by the way, a gyratory system of some fierceness – the motorist may continue southwards along the Rhône valley to Avignon, unless he wishes to turn east and pick up what the French call the Winter Route at Aspres-sur-Buech and so through Digne to Nice or Cannes. As I am dealing with this route in a later itinerary, I shall assume that we keep to the Rhône basin, making for the Riviera proper viâ Aix-en-Provence.

Should it be more convenient as to time one may be well advised to run on through Valence and lunch at Loriol, 20 kilometres further south. For, at the Restaurant à la Gondole, just outside the village to the north, appetite may be agreeably tickled and hunger comfortably stayed.

This wayside eating-house is quite new, having only been opened in the winter of 1930. The proprietress – Madame Beylon – has rebuilt and charmingly decorated an old farm-house and has (which is after all the main thing) a competent cook. The specialities of the house are:

        Bouillabaisse
        Langouste à l'Armoricaine
        Quenelles Nantua
        Tripes à la Mode de Caen
        Coq au Vin de Bourgogne

The set meal is 18 francs – for which I lunched as follows:
>   Hors-d'œuvres
>   Gibelotte de Garenne
>   Artichauts au Beurre
>   Côte d'Agneau garnie
>   Fromage
>   Dessert

It was well worth the money.

The first town of importance after Valence is Montélimar, 45 kilometres further south. Its staple industry is, of course, nougat. One can eat more nougat in a day in Montélimar, than one can see in a year anywhere else – if one wants to. There is also an aerodrome outside the town. The place used to be famous – or infamous – for the poorness of its entertainment for travellers (nougat always excepted), but a new hotel has recently been built outside the southern gate of the town, the which I can conscientiously recommend both to the Hungry and the Luxurious. The last time I stayed in Montélimar, before this hotel – the Relais de l'Empereur – was built, was at one of the older houses. It was as bad as it always had been, and I would not recall it now, but that it had a contraption at the porter's desk, in the form of an aid to memory, new to me – namely a board, fitted with hooks, in which each hook was numbered with hours and the divisions thereof. The porter, therefore, had only to hang the guest's key upon the hook corresponding to the hour at which he wished to be called. I had arrived late, and while the night porter had gone off in search of something for me to drink, I was unable to resist the temptation of changing several of the keys. I left early next morning and I have not been to this hotel since. Well, well – I was younger then than I am now – but I have always wished to see the faces of the couple who were down to be called at ten with a complete breakfast awakened at four without.

All this, however, is not of much practical help to the traveller, unless he be a Comic Traveller, who wishes to play with keys, and I expect they have abandoned this ingenious system by now, anyway. There is nothing like it at the Hôtel du Relais, a thoroughly modern house. It is more than that. It is one of the exceptions that prove the rule as to hôtels de luxe. The philosophically minded will remember, no doubt, that while man has always been carnivorous, he has only quite recently become clean. Not so long ago, he was content to sleep on a pallet after eating a poulet from the spit and to wash himself at the pump before sitting down to a meal such as we cannot even see to-day, let alone pay for. Comfort is apt to kill the kitchen, as sanitation, the cellar. It is true the Romans had baths as well as banquets – but that was before my time.

But to return to the present. The table at the Relais is as good as one might expect in a much humbler house. A large and convenient garage, modern decoration and an American bar have in no way threatened the proper satisfaction of the Hungry Traveller. This may, in part, be due to the restaurant being managed – and for all I know, owned – apart from the hotel, by one of the most famous (if not the most famous) of Lyon restaurants – the Morateur. The name alone is symptomatic of the highest culinary art. The last time

THE LOWER RHÔNE

I stayed there I enjoyed a cream soup, a trout meunière, cardons au gratin and a guinea-fowl with mushrooms. I also drank one of the best bottles of Rhône wine I have tasted for years – namely a bottle of Côte Rotie, of 1904, from Morateur's reserved cuvée.

I do not advise the bar. It is beautiful to look at, but the barman is generally not there – which is by far the best place for him.

Fifty-two kilometres from Montélimar brings you to Orange: a town famous for an amphitheatre, bad hotels, black troops, crystallised fruits, truffles and a triumphal arch. The last named is unmistakable, as you have to drive round it to enter the town – not through it, unless you are being received by the Mayor – and I dare say not even then. Other points of interest can be seen by the curious without much trouble. There is, however, at least one good restaurant in Orange – the Hôtel Moderne. The house has two set meals, one at 16 and one at 20 francs. The latter one, the last time I fed there, was as follows:

> Hors-d'œuvres (really excellent)
> Rouget meunière
> Petits Pois à la Français
> Poulet rôti
> Salade
> Fromages
> Dessert

One should, however, be warned to feed early, as the Moderne is, locally, very popular.

If the traveller has slept at Montélimar (we will suppose a gentle stage of some 120 kilometres) he may be advised to lunch at Châteauneuf-du-Pape. If, after these three meals, he is not dead (or dying) he may be decorated with the Grand Order of Gastronomy – Second Class. I myself, I may say in parenthesis, hold the First Class – with bar; but it is not given to every one to achieve such distinction; and I duly warn the less courageous against lightly attempting Châteauneuf-du-Pape; at least, on a full stomach. It presents the epicure with a pleasant little repast of some nine courses, none of which are easy to refuse.

From Orange to Châteauneuf is only some 10 kilometres. One takes G.C.70 and, later, G.C.57. The eating-house is the Hôtel Bellevue – and is most appropriately named, for one dines on a terrace overlooking the valley of the Rhône and half a dozen departments. There are two set meals – (yes, you are right, last time I was there I ate the larger) which was, as far as I remember, as follows:

> Hors-d'œuvres variés
> Pâté de la Maison (3 or 4 kinds)
> Écrevisse à l'Armoricaine
> Omelette truffé
> Rognons madères
> Bécasse flambée
> Salade
> Crème Chocolat
> Fromages
> Fruits

This meal costs (or cost) 35 francs. It is well worth the money if you have both the time and capacity to enjoy it. It is not to be forgotten that Châteauneuf-du-Pape grows a wine of the same name. There are a number of vineyards, owned by a variety of pro-

THE LOWER RHÔNE 75

prietors. To my own taste, I have found the Clos St.-Pierre (Prosper Quiot) and the Clos du Pape most agreeable; and have found them preferable to many mediocre (or, perhaps, so-called) Burgundies. From Châteauneuf-du-Pape to Avignon is 17 kilometres. One cuts into N.7, just outside Sorgues – a somewhat dismal place, devoted to chemical works and the like. There is a tramway from there to Avignon and I saw – the last time I passed that way – a whole furniture van upset (and its varied contents scattered) upon it. I met a crowded tram later hastening unconsciously towards the scene of disaster. I often wondered what happened, for you cannot remove a tram from its lines or a demolished furniture van from them either, in a hurry. Avignon itself, I do my best to avoid; which can easily be done by a by-pass road (G.C.81) which gives the town a wide berth, picking up N.7 some 6 kilometres on the other side. If the traveller must needs see the Palace of the Popes and all the other jolly things to be seen there, he can stay, comfortably, at the Dominion Hotel and pay accordingly; or he can stay at other hotels and be a little less comfortable, at much the same price. Of the eating-houses there I know nothing. M. Hiély – who owned the restaurant of that name there, is a personal friend of mine. But he has long since left the town and retired elsewhere. I shall have something to say of M. Hiély later. There may be (indeed I know, from private evidence, that there are) hotels and restaurants still unspoilt, in Avignon. But the vast tourist traffic is, in this town, so omnipresent, that it has always sickened me of the place; and so deterred me from searching out those petits coins intimes, the which, in this welter of Cookisme, are all the more to be cherished and preserved.

I notice that Mr. Karl Baedeker says the mistral is sometimes trying here. I cannot but admire his reticence.

CHAPTER SEVEN

PROVENCE

The direct route for the traveller from Avignon to Nice is still on N.7, through Aix-en-Provence, Brignoles and Cannes – which road indeed only ends at the Italian frontier at Garavan. If, however, the weather be fine, and the traveller wishes to see some of the wildest and most beautiful scenery in France, he will be well advised to take N.100 out of Avignon to Apt and Manosque and thence, by a series of roads to be detailed later, to Castellane, where he drops into the main road to Grasse. I should very strongly advise the epicure taking this road to stop for lunch at Gordes. If he has stopped the night at Montélimar, he can very comfortably do this in a morning's run, lunching at Gordes instead of at Châteauneuf-du-Pape. In this instance, he follows the main road N.7, as far as the cross-roads just outside Avignon and then takes the 'loop' road, G.C.87, until it cuts N.100, about a kilometre further on. One turns east and follows this main road some 30 kilometres until one reaches the cross-roads at Coustellet. One turns left here into G.C.75, seven kilometres bringing one to Gordes. The total run is about 110 kilometres. One can alternately take the loop road through Carpentras; but little is to be gained by doing this.

Gordes itself is one of the most picturesque little towns in the south of France, built, as it is, on the summit of a sudden and steep hill, stuck out of the plain, and dominated by its ancient castle. It also boasts one of the best restaurants for its size anywhere. This is the Hôtel de la Renaissance, and the Hungry Traveller must on no account miss it. It is the tiniest place, but do not be discouraged by its appearance. You will find sawdust on the floor and you may or may not be honoured with a table-cloth. Arrive in good time and consult M. Pantaly-Gentil as to your meal. The true epicure should be enough of a cook to know that certain dishes take time to prepare and many cannot be served unless arranged for beforehand.

The last time I lunched at Gordes I ate as follows:

> Pâté de grives
> Truite meunière
> Omelette Champignon
> Perdreaux rôtis
> Salade
> Gâteau Maison
> Fromages
> Fruits

I have seldom tasted better cooking. The thrush pâté was a real delight, and M. Pantaly-Gentil is also a genius who can roast. The cake – a speciality of the house – is to be specially noticed. The best wine to drink there is the Châteauneuf.

On the other side of the main road, opposite Gordes,

is Cavaillon – the very heart of the early vegetable market. Although a small town of only some seven thousand inhabitants all told, the population is so rich that the place supports a number of gambling clubs – properly licensed, of course – and cultivators in corduroy will win or lose fortunes in a night. It is probably unique as being the only gambling centre in France where the Anglo-Saxon is unknown. I once tried – and failed – to find a place to eat there. Doubtless one is oneself too much in the very heart of the cauliflower to swallow it.

On leaving Gordes to move eastward, one should take the left-hand road off G.C.75, just outside the village – a road of the category V.O. – which stands for Voie Ordinaire, and not Very Odd, as sometimes might seem to be the case. This brings one into N.100 some 8 kilometres further east than where one left it. Thence, keeping on N.100 as far as Reillanne and then turning into N.207, some 60 kilometres brings one to Manosque.

Manosque is a delightful old-world town, quite unspoilt by the tourist; and the Hôtel Pascal there is one of the most agreeable houses I know – alike for the comfort of its rooms and the cordiality of its welcome, as for its service and its food.

On leaving Manosque, one first crosses the Durance on N.207, but instead of following the national route to the left, one keeps straight on, on G.C.6, to Valensole. Then begins one of the loveliest runs I know of anywhere – that is, if one is fond of wild and rocky scenery.

The road climbs all the way up from the river to Moustiers-St.-Marie – this picturesque town being at an altitude of 2000 feet, and 1000 feet above Manosque. From Moustiers, one follows G.C.6 for 2 kilometres and then forking right into G.C.2, winds up above the Grand Cañon of the Verdon to a height of over 3000 feet. The finest view-point is at Rougon (2400 feet), where one gazes almost vertically down into the Cañon. I scarcely know of a finer piece of scenery of its kind in France than this. It appears to be almost unknown to the English. It is well worth the slight difficulties of getting there; and it might be as well, here, to warn the motorist as to the road – especially from Rougon down into Castellane. It is one of the most dangerous roads I know, having a blank cliff face one side and a thousand-foot precipice the other, with an apology of a parapet here and there. As all the corners are blind and one turns completely round every hundred yards and the road will only accommodate one vehicle – except at arranged passing places – I suggest to the prudent motorist that this is not a suitable track for speed records.

From Rougon to Castellane is only some 15 kilometres. But as I am dealing later with Castellane, and the so-called Winter Road upon which it is situated, I shall return now to the other and more direct route to Nice.

In this case, one has to follow the by-pass road, mentioned above, across N.100 until N.7 is reached – a matter of another 4 kilometres. One follows this south-eastward, the Durance being crossed by the suspension bridge at Bompas. From Avignon to Aix is one of the finest roads in France to travel on, provided the mistral is not blowing, in which case a moderation in speed is to be advised, since the mistral blows in gusts and is apt to take a fast car into the ditch. The road is wide, straight and open; and this lap of 75 kilometres can comfortably be accomplished in an hour and a half – Bentley or Bugatti owners and the like, will, of course, do it in much less time. One should beware of the level crossings, in some of which the rails are not so flat with the road as they appear.

There is little in the way of entertainment to incite the traveller to stop before he reaches Aix. I once ate one of the poorest meals in my life at Senas; and I have been advised personally, of the excellence of the Lion d'Or at Lambesc – 20 kilometres before Aix; but I know of this only from hearsay. At Aix-en-Provence itself one can do a number of things. One can, for instance, take the waters, internally or externally – hot or cold. One can also play Boule, Chemin-de-fer and Baccarat at the local casino between October and June. A great hotel has recently been built there, of the very latest comfort and luxury, where one can (according to Michelin) pay as much as 250 francs a night for a room, if one is so minded. There are also other hotels in the town with more moderate charges, though, of course, not so luxurious.

The Sextius (with which is incorporated the baths) used to be – I have not been there since '27 – a comfortable house, with an excellent kitchen; the meals tending, however, to be somewhat large and lengthy. No doubt, very necessary qualities: though it has always been a moot point in my mind as to whether the meals were planned to satisfy the bathers – or the baths installed for the amelioration of the diners. One can also dine at the Casino. I only dined there once myself and do not propose to do so again. I have it, on good authority, that they can cook at the Hôtel Riviera, but I have not personally eaten there.

I would particularly recommend the epicure, mobile with a motor car, to adventure 6 kilometres outside the town to Tholonet. The more especially if it be summer-time (Aix can be miserably cold in the winter) and one can eat out of doors.

This restaurant – the Thomé – at Tholonet is pleasantly situated among trees – under which one dines. The cooking is of the first class and à la carte. The curious will note a marble slab set in the wall of the house announcing the not uninteresting fact that a M. Gras drove King Edward vii there on a particular date. I am having a similar stone cut to announce the fact that I also drove an illustrious personage there not long ago, but I am keeping the matter incognito until the stone is up.

From Aix to Brignoles is 57 kilometres; and I would urge the Epicurean and the Luxurious to stop at least for a meal, if not for a night, at the Tivoli, at the latter place. There are few pleasanter hotels or better kitchens in the South of France. It is another of those rare exceptions to the rule – like the Relais at Montélimar – a thoroughly up-to-date and modern house, that still preserves the tradition of good cooking. It is also – it may be remembered by the way – most conveniently situated for the traveller passing through from Montélimar to Nice: allotting him 210 kilometres in the morning (but on the best of roads) and a more modest run of 130 in the afternoon.

There is a set meal at 35 francs, and I happen to have by me two menus: one of 21st July and the other

of 26th October – both of last year. The former reads as follows:
>Hors-d'œuvres
>Rouget de roche meunière
>ou
>Écrevisses à la brignolaisse
>Poulet grain rôti
>Pommes rissolées
>Céleries en branches au beurre
>Fromages
>Glace vanille
>Gauffrettes
>Fruits

and the latter:
>Hors-d'œuvres
>Terrine maison
>Omelette aux truffes
>Caneton poché molière
>Pommes étuvées
>Choux-fleurs sautés au beurre
>Fromages
>Crème au caramel
>Fruits

The specialities of the house are:
>Truites, au bleu ou meunière
>Châteaubriand aux pommes
>Écrevisses, and
>Crêpes Suzette

The last time I dined there I drank an admirable bottle of Vergelesses – of '19.

The next stepping-off place for the gourmet that I know of is le Luc-en-Provence, 24 kilometres further on. I have known the Hôtel du Parc for years and I have a feeling that latterly it has deteriorated perceptibly – but it may well be, simply, that I am growing old. The proprietor will receive you with open arms and speaks (for the benefit of transatlantic travellers) American as well as French. His kitchen is excellent; and, if the weather be clement, his garden is delightful to dine in. I can recommend his truite meunière and especially his grives provençales – if you are fond of garlic. I have tasted no better grives provençales elsewhere – with the one exception of those of M. Hiély, in his retreat: but it is no dishonour to give place to M. Hiély. Do not, however, have foisted on you here – or anywhere else – the Varois wine called Camp Romain. It is not worth the price asked for it, much of which, I think, must go in réclame. To my own taste, all Varois wines are poor – at least, I lived in this department for years without finding a really drinkable one.

You can also eat humbly – but well and cheaply – at Vidauban, 10 kilometres further on from le Luc.

From le Luc to Fréjus is a matter of 38 kilometres. Here one can either keep to the coast, through St.-Raphael, on N.7, coming into Cannes through la Napoule; or cut inland across the Esterel. The latter is the shorter road by some 9 kilometres and a better one for the motorist. One misses the seascape, but one has the mountains instead. I have been unable, of late, to find a place to feed at in Fréjus. There was not a bad restaurant there some years ago, but it is now a cinema. It also contains the ruins of one of the biggest amphitheatres in France, and detachments of the blackest of black troops. Motorists unfamiliar with these Colonials should remember that what the psychologists call the 'time-reaction' is, with the 'Maroc,' extremely slow.

Blowing your horn is often a futile pastime; and it is always safer to go round a Maroc than to expect a Maroc to go round you.

Thirty-five kilometres, by the Esterel road, brings the traveller to the English Colony of Cannes.

If, however, the weather be clement and the traveller be wishful of avoiding the main through roads of N.7 and N.97, he may well be advised to take the upper loop road from Brignoles, viâ Draguignan. He can then either continue on the upper road to Grasse, and thence direct to Nice or cut down to N.7 at le Muy. To do this, one takes G.C.120, to the north of Brignoles, through Lorgues to Draguignan – a matter of 45 kilometres. If one wishes to spend a little time in the present capital of the Var, one may profitably do so, without incurring any gastronomic hardship. I advise the epicure to shun the hotels and lunch at the Buffet de la Gare, taking his apéro' first at the Brasserie Alsacienne in the centre of the town. He must not be discouraged by the outward appearance of the Buffet. It looks (and is) but a humble place, yet the food is of the best. I remember making a very pleasant little meal there of hors-d'œuvres (the home-made brawn was peculiarly delightful) caneloni – cooked as it can be done in Italy itself – roast veal and potatoes, cheese and fruit. I drank some agreeable Cornas and Marc (Chambolle-Musigny) afterwards.

To return to N.7 at le Muy is only a short run of 12 kilometres. Otherwise, one continues by G.C.120 (later G.C.34) to Grasse and thence, by N.85, to Cagnes and Nice. The total distance from Draguignan to Nice by this route is 94 kilometres, or to Cannes, 74.

CHAPTER EIGHT

TOM TIDDLER'S GROUND

The coast from Cannes to the Italian frontier – or even from St.-Raphael – is, of course, settled and visited almost exclusively by the English and the American. It is true that prosperous Germans go to Nice and every nationality, black, yellow and white, is to be seen at Monte Carlo. But the vast bulk of the foreigner in these parts is Anglo-Saxon. You may occasionally see a Frenchman at Nice – in the neighbourhood of the station.

It might well be thought superfluous – I had almost said impertinent – to inform your travelled Englishman, in any way, about this department of the Maritime Alps, the which he has made so particularly his own. He might well be presumed to know all there is to know there – at any rate, in respect to the less recondite curricula of eating and drinking. But after more than ten years' careful scrutiny of my fellow-countrymen abroad, I have come to the conclusion that the English are very like sheep. At least, the hordes of English that go to the Riviera are. They are pitifully afraid of getting lost from the flock.

This is all to the good. For it effectively segregates the great mass of tourists into certain well-known hotels and casinos; leaving, even on this exploited coast, some hinterland for the more egregious of us to explore and enjoy. Indeed this demarcation is so remarkable that, at Nice, for instance, I have never seen a Frenchman in the bar of the Ruhl – save the barman, and he's an Italian; yet I have never seen an Englishman in the Cintra – a bare quarter of a mile away.

Moreover, even places peculiarly known to the English are liable to change – more so, perhaps, on the Azur coast than anywhere else; and the latest information is always of value as far as it goes. Lastly, and by no means least, we are, every one of us, sadly creatures of habit. In places familiar to us we are very apt to confine ourselves to a particular hotel, a particular restaurant and a particular bar. Custom is strong in us; and like Hamlet, we are ready to bear with the discomforts and extortions that we know, rather than fly to others that we know not of. Few of us know all the eating-houses in a large town – I myself most emphatically do not – and the few I know and can recommend may well be unknown to my neighbour.

The first place of any importance one reaches after leaving the Var, is, of course, Cannes. Its reputation was made by Lord Brougham, who settled there in 1834, and the town has remained an appanage of the English ever since. It has two casinos – a winter one and a summer one. The latter, under the able and genial direction of M. Chauvelet – one of the most delightful of hosts – really has a kitchen; and provides one with a remarkably good meal – at, of course, current casino prices.

While speaking of establishments de luxe with a purely English clientèle, I think it only fair to say that the Majestic Grill (only open in winter) is, in my opinion, the second best grill on the Riviera – the first being that of the Ruhl at Nice, of the same administration. The charges are proportionate. One must be content (in full season) to lunch in the company of loud-voiced women, complete with lap-dogs and male appendices, but one cannot mix in Riviera Society without paying the necessary price for it.

One can, strange as it may seem, eat well in Cannes, without being harassed by pyjama-wearers in the summer and the boiled shirters in the winter and the general ruck of Suburbia on holiday. I do not say that you will find no English at Robert's. One could scarcely hope for that – in Cannes. But such as go there are essentially epicureans and (it is to be hoped) Gentle Travellers. One goes to Robert's to eat – not to see what Lady X has (or has not) got on or to scrape up an acquaintance with Lord Y, over an imported whisky. One even goes there simply to eat and to enjoy it at the time.

For the benefit of such of the Hungry as do not know Robert's, I will indicate that it is a humble-looking place, opposite the station, at the corner of the rue Serbe. Its menu is à la carte, and, indeed, it possesses one of the most complete bills of fare I have found outside the gastronomic capitals. Nor is its list in any way 'chichis.' What is there detailed you can really and truly have; rightly and strictly cooked, in accord with the classic tradition of French cookery. I particularly call to the notice of the gourmet the hors-d'œuvres, which are numerous and varied, beautifully (and I may say generously) served — as also (an important matter, not everywhere observed) straight off the ice. Among them, I especially esteem the black olives. It is only in a few houses where you may find really good black olives; the curing of these being (as the northerners may not know) an intricate process; olive 'vintages' being as cherished as those of the grape. I can also remember, in this category, their pimentoes and their cêpes. The last time I dined there I ordered myself a comfortable little meal of hors-d'œuvres, roast partridge, and wild strawberries. I drank with it a bottle of Lanson '18; in my opinion, a very notable wine, and one difficult to find in most restaurants. Do not suppose that because the English have never heard of it (or don't like it) that you may therefore get it cheap. You won't. You'll be lucky to find it at a pound a bottle. The generalisation so often made that you can only drink good champagne in England is about as stupid as saying you can only drink good whisky in Wales. Champagne, like whisky, is blended to suit a local and prevailing taste.

And while I am still concerned with what I might call the snobismo complices of the English diner-out (a subject not unsuitable to Cannes) let me, for Heaven's sake, explode the fatuous dogma that you cannot drink champagne throughout a meal. I am content to note that Mr. Berry records a champagne dinner in his delightful book and that M. de Cassignac very properly admits the practice. Indeed, almost anything may be drunk throughout a properly designed meal. People have even been known to drink water. . . .

I see in my Michelin that there are at least two restaurants in Cannes worthy of two stars and two dots — the which indicates houses replete with 'every up-to-date comfort.' I fear I am ignorant of both of them; but I feel sure the Britisher can dine there quite comfortably in the very best company — and even wear a white tie. Don't wear a white tie at Robert's. Not that they would be in any way rude to you, but they might mistake you for the band.

The traveller may go from Cannes to Nice by the main road in a little under an hour, dependent on the traffic, and his escaping unscathed over the worst-driven stretch of road in the world — at least in the English season. Or he may turn off either to Juan-les-Pins or Cap d'Antibes on the way. I am afraid I know little of either. I once tried to bathe at one of them, but I was too fat to get in — space being strictly limited. I have lunched among the lions — out of curiosity. The late Mr. W. J. Locke was in the habit of saying that the place was too full of fair men and brave women for his own taste. I think his criticism moderate. I certainly shall not lunch there again — the close proximity of semi-naked Nordics having small appeal to me. It is, if I remember rightly, this hotel that is famous for its hors-d'œuvres ingeniously (if a little ingenuously) composed of six different dishes, repeated six times. But then, after all, you can eat them in bathing-drawers: which, of course, covers a multitude of sins. . . . Leaving such heliotherapists — I presume they must be that, to put up with such overcrowding and underfeeding – one arrives, in due course, at Nice.

I am not fond of this Mediterranean Brighton, but I prefer it to Cannes – Robert's always excepted. Of course, that is not saying much – Cannes, as it were, being Bournemouth (or perhaps Boscombe?). Any man in his senses would prefer Brighton – it is more vulgar. At least Nice is vulgar, in the right sense of that misunderstood word, as in the wrong. One might starve in Nice, when one would have to steal at Cannes. Of restaurants in Nice (not being in love with the place) I know only four, apart from the cosmopolitan hotels. My own habit is for a small and humble house, scarcely a hundred yards off the Promenade of the English, the name of which, like Edward Gibbon, in another matter, I have forgotten. It is within two minutes' walk of the gardens of King Albert the First, and, if you are clever, you can easily find it for yourself. The second is the Poularde, just behind the Galeries Lafayette. You can eat here (it is a Lyonnais house) the most excellent quenelles and poularde au gros sel as well as anywhere outside Lyon. You will have to endure some singing – and even story-telling – the which is included free of charge. It might well appeal to a deaf Scotsman – otherwise, one can only recommend patience and cotton-wool. The third is the Caressa; an old-fashioned, but agreeable house, with, perhaps, the second best grill in Nice. It also has a comfortable bar where one can take one's apéro' while waiting for the grill. I can also speak highly of the Français just off the Place Massena. There is a table-d'hôte there, au choix; but I recommend a choice à la carte. The last time I ate there, I had a langouste, followed by a spring chicken, green peas and salad – all admirable. As for the above noted petit coin, I feel sure that the Gentle, the Modest and the Ingenious Traveller will easily discover it for himself. When he has found it and enjoyed it, he will do just as I have done – and, that is, not give it away to anybody else.

There are three roads by which one can go from Nice to Mentone. The family man may take the uppermost – or Grande Corniche – and so escape the snares (long since rusted away) of Monte Carlo. The more adventurous may go to Monaco either by the Moyenne Corniche, and so enjoy not only the view from Eze, but also the local engineer's inverted theory of road-banking or one may take the lower road – the Corniche Inférieure – viâ Villefranche and Beaulieu and the tramlines. Of the big and middle Corniches, I have nothing to report in the way of gastronomic adventure. But if the Hungry Traveller takes the Lower One, and turns off, after Villefranche, into the tiny peninsula of Cap Ferrat, on any day between the 27th October and the 10th of May, he should at least feel some premonition of his fate. For he will be in speaking distance, almost, of the High Altar of Gastronomy and the living presence of the Grand Master of all Cooks. Need I say that I speak of Caramello?

I spoke, in an earlier chapter, of the Grand Master Cook of France. In my experience and opinion, at least, M. Caramello is that man. He is the greatest chef de la cuisine that I know of. It might well be thought that all England knows of him, since in the summer months he opens his restaurant at Aix-les-Bains. But although (I take it) only the English go to Aix-les-

Bains, all Englishmen do not go there – I don't myself, for instance, having a rooted dislike to being shut in by mountains, drinking water and wasting my money for the name of the thing. So there may yet be many who do not know the name of Caramello.

His restaurant at St.-Jean-Cap-Ferrat (I know nothing of his Aix-les-Bains house) is a small and modest-looking place. But it is pleasantly situated overlooking the sea.

M. Caramello's 'specialities' might well fill a volume – for he can cook anything and everything. One may particularise his hors-d'œuvres – which total some sixty in number, all different, unlike at another place – the first series being cold ones and the second hot.

If, after half an hour or so, toying with these incomparably excellent dishes, one has capacity to eat any more (one should go into training for Caramello's) his baby lobsters, cooked in sea-water, are as near heaven, in the fish line, as you are likely to find in this world. After that, a tiny lamb – roasted whole – may be indicated. I really do not know how and where M. Caramello finds such diminutive and delicious animals – I have never seen or eaten such lambs elsewhere – but they are (like the lobsters) a privilege to eat. As I once overheard a Frenchman say to his wife there, after entirely devouring one of these quadrupeds between them – 'Caramello's may be dear, but it is really cheap in the long run – since one need eat nothing for a week afterwards!' Yes: you will even find Frenchmen going there, and suffering an English clientèle – and it takes damn' good food to make a Frenchman do that!

YOU CAN CATCH YOUR OWN FISH

One could expound for hours upon the genius of Caramello. I really know no hyperbole too extravagant for his table – unless something terrible has happened since I was there last. It is invidious, even, to cite particular dishes. Choose to your taste and you will be more than satisfied. One cannot, however, omit to mention, specifically, the crêpes Suzettes – for at Caramello's only have I found such a pancake made, as it should be made – that is, of the weight and texture of fine lace. M. Caramello will serve you these pancakes, each in turn cooked in the chafing-dish with a different liqueur. My own record is a series of nine, in the following order, if my memory is not at fault: Marasquino, Cointreau, Prunelle, Kirsch, Kummel, Absinthe (Pernod), Grand Marnier, Chartreuse, and fine Champagne.

You may drink with your meal an excellent white wine – en carafe – at the modest price of some 15 francs a bottle. Otherwise, M. Caramello's cellar is fully worthy of his kitchen.

To leave Cap Ferrat for other places, is bound to be, for the gourmet, in the nature of a declension. But one may not with a normally constituted stomach live for ever upon the mountain-tops.

On the lower road to Monte Carlo, one passes through Beaulieu and may feed at the Reserve there. It has a great reputation among the visitors to the Riviera; but a good deal of it (I fancy) is due to the fact that you choose the fish which you are going to eat as it swims or crawls about in the fountain outside.

At Monte Carlo, one need not, of course, starve –

at least, provided one has not lost all one's money at the tables.

The best restaurant in Monte Carlo (and the most expensive) is, probably, Ciro's – the Ambassador's running it a close second. Both these are only open in the winter season, and are too well known to invite remark.

I would rank Quinto's next – and, for the diner, who wishes to eat without the external aids of music and dress clothes, peculiarly to be recommended. The prices are inclined to be high; but the food is excellent: although I shall take the occasion here to remark that the service is apt to be somewhat perfunctory – except just before tipping time.

There is one restaurant in Monte Carlo deserving of very special notice – namely Stalle's, down upon the quay. One should lunch there when the weather is such as to permit of outdoor eating. No epicure is likely to be disappointed with Stalle. His dishes are really excellent and his prices moderate. The last time I lunched there, I ate a dish of fresh tunny, garlic, rice, and black olives of a remarkable delicacy. But do not go there on boat days!

One used to be able, some ten years ago, to eat well at the Café de Paris, but the sad process of the demoralisation of Monte Carlo has reduced this once excellent and agreeable restaurant to much the same level as the popular houses of entertainment in London, affected by the jeunesse dorée of Tooting and Raynes Park. Such gay sparks as now go to 'good old Monte' in order to say that they have been there, will no doubt go to the 'good old Café de Paris' for much the same reason. After all – 'tout change, tout passe' – il faut être philosophe – and this reason is no doubt as good as any other. . . .

Of the smaller and more modest restaurants in Monte Carlo, at least four deserve (or deserved) mention. For the price charged for a meal (it used to be 15 francs) the Napolitain gave excellent value for the outlay involved. The same might be said of the Giardino. What used to be known locally as 'Pam's' (I think it is now called Albert's) was once, when owned by Mr. Savile, a remarkably good place in which to take a light lunch – but I understand he has since sold it, and as they so often say in the 'Club-sans-Club,' I have no renseignements for 1931. One other place I can recommend from past experience – and that is, the Brasserie Royale: if it still be open. I remember it as a quiet and unfrequented restaurant with quite good cooking à la carte.

From Monte Carlo to Menton is only a matter of a few minutes by car, and one passes almost imperceptibly from the fevered aura of octogenarian gaiety into the quiet waters of septuagenarian repose. I once stayed three weeks in Menton, but I do not propose, unless I am bound to, to stay there again. Perhaps the atmosphere is enervating.

There are at least two restaurants in Menton with a big name, which scintillate (as to stars in Michelin) like the constellation of the Bear. I regret I have no experience of either of them. While in Menton, I stayed (and ate) at a tiny hotel on the road to Sospel – the Merle Blanc. Of this little house and its wide terrace I have the happiest recollections. And I can

A MONTE CARLO IDYLL

commend to the notice both of the Hungry and of the Humane Traveller, M. Baulet, the proprietor (and, happily, also, the cook) of this delightful little retreat from Suburbia-on-Sea. He is not only a great cook but a great personality. He speaks, at least, four languages – French (real French, not Marseillaise), American, German and Italian – he probably speaks three or four more tongues, but I was unable, myself, to test him further. At any rate, he has travelled all over the world – a rare thing in a true Frenchman – and you must get him to start (and stop) telling you some of his stories – preferably in French. The latter requires more tact than the former.

It is needless to add (I was actually content to stay there en pension) that his cooking is admirable; and you will be well advised, sometimes, to order one of his specialities and ignore the expense: it is not great, in any case.

A few hundred yards beyond Menton, one comes to the end of France. It is outside the provenance of these notes to speak of Italy – interesting as the subject is to any gourmet: in many ways, of more interest than France, where so much is known, and too much (unhappily) slave to fashion and a formula. To the true adventurers in gastronomy, there are few countries more entertaining than Italy, provided the epicure can speak the language (in many cases the dialect); is ready to put up with some trifling discomforts and avoids any hotels frequented by the English (or Germans) as he would the devil.

Two eating-houses, however, actually in Italy, but only five minutes' walk across the border, may be of some interest to the visitor to Menton. They are the Roches Rouges – on the sea road, which is really a cul-de-sac: you are allowed to take your car there, without going through the tryptich or carnet de douane formalities; and Grimaldi, next to the Italian customs on the main road – to be reached à pied unless you wish to take your car into Italy. In the former, M. Abbo will allow you to catch your own crayfish in the cave underneath his restaurant. At Grimaldi, you will be able to hear a blind violinist imitate a dog with amazing verisimilitude. You will eat equally well in both places; as to entertainment, you can take your choice.

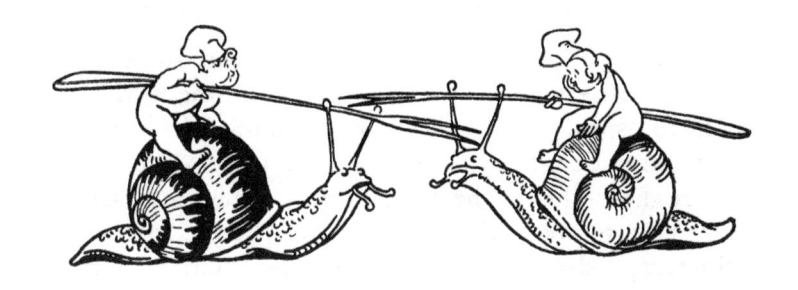

SECOND JOURNEY – UP

CHAPTER NINE

THE WINTER ROUTE

Why the road to the south, viâ Grenoble, Sisteron and Digne should be called the Route d'Hiver has always been something of a mystery to me. One would have imagined that the Rhône valley road, through Aix-en-Provence, would have been more properly named as the road for the Winter Traveller. It is true that this road is kept officially 'open' throughout the winter months – that is to say, it is cleared by the snow-plough whenever necessary; for one of the highest points on the road is the Col de la Croix-Haute (3630 feet) and heavy falls of snow may occur here. I have crossed it without chains in December, but one should always have chains with one in taking this road in winter-time. With the Saône and Rhône valley route, the risk of snow is, of course, negligible once one has dropped down from the high plateau of the Morvan. However, whatever time of year, the Route d'Hiver, or the Route des Alpes, is a very lovely one: but the ideal time to take it is in the spring, when the flowers are out. It does not only offer delights to the eye, but always the more material delights of the table; for, as a rule, they know well how to cook in the Dauphiné. In the following itinerary, I shall trace the journey from south to north.

Starting from Nice, there are two loops to Digne, one being, as far as time goes, about as long as the other. One may pass viâ Puget-Théniers, or viâ Castellane. To take the former first, one turns north, a little way out of Nice on the west, into N.202 (unless one wishes to take N.209, on the other side of the river as far as St. Martin-du-Var). Sixty-four kilometres brings one to Puget-Théniers, a rather shabby-looking town of some twelve hundred inhabitants, offering (I should imagine) little of interest to the Epicurean Traveller.

Seven kilometres on from Puget, one comes to one of the most picturesque towns in France – namely Entrevaux. It is well worth while to leave the car outside for a moment and cross the drawbridge to look more closely into this unspoilt little place. It has a restaurant, with a terrace overlooking the river, but I have never eaten there myself.

At 20 kilometres from Puget and 84 from Nice is the fork to Barcelonnette. To continue to Digne, one crosses the river to the left. If one has only made a lazy morning's run from Nice, the traveller cannot do better than follow up the Barcelonnette fork for a couple of kilometres into the quaint little hill town of Annot and lunch there at the Hôtel Philip. I myself was sent there by M. Morel (of Digne), of whom more later. M. Morel well knows what is good cooking: it is needless to say that M. Philip does also. The hotel is also pleasantly situated and spotlessly clean. The set lunch for the day, at 16 francs, is admirable. I drank some of the local Marc, which was remarkably good, of its kind: those who know what locally distilled Marc can be like, and how seldom it is drinkable, will appreciate this recommendation. Should one wish to make a longer morning's run of it, one can lunch well at St.-André-les-Alpes, 110 kilometres from Nice; at the Hôtel du Parc in the little square near the church. The proprietor at one time cooked at the Grand Hôtel in Monte Carlo – and his table at the Parc is excellent. It is also a comfortable little house at which to stay the night.

St.-André to Barrème is 13 kilometres, where the other loop road comes in from Castellane. Should the traveller wish to take this road, he takes N.7 as far as Cagnes, there branching off to the right into N.85, he will pass through Grasse where the scents are made and, if the wind is blowing in the right direction, be able to enjoy the smell of their manufacture, which is a cross between that of a tannery and a tallow-refining factory.

The observant traveller will, on his way up to Grasse from Nice notice glaring posters at every turn of the road, imploring him to eat at the Rôtisserie of La Reine Pédauque. This feverish publicity has not, so far, succeeded in inducing me to find out if the proprietor of the house has any money left over to spend on food, but the curious, anxious to settle the point, will have no difficulty in finding the place. Apart from this pictorial appeal, I fear I know nothing, gastronomically, about Grasse.

From Nice to Grasse is 38 kilometres; and another 64 kilometres brings one to Castellane. The latter part of the road is extremely fine, the road reaching a height of nearly 4000 feet.

Castellane itself is a most fascinating place to look at; and conversely (to-day) a most miserable place to eat in. There are only two hotels – the one no better than the other. It is, I imagine, a place sadly given over to sightseers in motor-'buses, and these monsters murder inns.

It is, indeed, a pity; for Castellane could once boast of an inn, worthy of the best traditions of inn-keeping. The last time I went there and entered it, I found things changed. I did not eat there, but after waiting some little time to be served (happily in vain) and noting the dishes served to my neighbours, I slipped out into the square. It was evident that M. X. no longer ran the place. I buttonholed a young man, who looked as if he belonged to the locality, and asked him where M. X. now had his restaurant.

'Je ne sais pas,' he said, politely, with a shrug of his shoulders, 'il est décédé.' Alas, there is a sad mortality among good hosts. . . .

I eventually lunched at the other hotel; and ate as poor a meal as I have eaten anywhere. But, at least, they had manners and did their best.

From Castellane to Barrême is 24 kilometres, and thence another 30 to Digne. Thus, from Nice to Digne, viâ Castellane, is 156 kilometres, and viâ Puget-Théniers, 152. If one wishes to push through, and do this stage in a morning, the latter is the road to be preferred; but one must bear in mind that the road is a dangerous one and a good four or five hours should be allowed for the run.

The first time I went to Digne I stopped at the roadside – some miles from it – to consult my map. A gentleman in a passing car kindly stopped, and learning that I proposed to stop the night in Digne, assured me, with much gesture and emphasis, that it was quite impossible to eat in that town. I may say that he was wrong; but I think I might have taken his assurances in better part if he had not gone on to inform me that if I only crossed the river, from where I was, to the small town of Volonne and put up at the hotel which he had the honour to own, I could, on the contrary, obtain the very perfection of bed and board. I do not know if this ingenuous gentleman still patrols the main road to try and divert travellers into Volonne. But I am glad to say that I remained unmoved by his entreaties and so was able to enjoy the agreeable hospitality of M. Morel, of the Grand Hôtel, at Digne.

You can eat well at Digne – at M. Morel's table: have no fear of that. I particularly remember his vol-au-vent and his vanilla soufflé. This house, also, is patronised by the townsfolk; which is always the highest recommendation of cooking.

There has recently been built, just outside the town, a modern and elaborate hotel, where (the 'Club-sans-Club' says) you can enjoy 'all the pleasures of the grand palaces.' They are discreetly silent as to the house's other attractions. No doubt, as 'Enery Straker said of

Eton and Harrow, it's very well for them as likes that sort of thing.

From Digne to Sisteron is only about 40 kilometres: of this interesting old town I know nothing, gastronomically speaking, though I have no doubt that search there would repay the adventurous.

From Sisteron to Grenoble, one has the choice of two routes; the direct way viâ Serres and Aspres and thence over the Col de la Croix-Haute – or the more circuitous route viâ Gap and the Col Bayard. As this col is some 400 feet higher than the former, the road by Serres is to be preferred – in winter-time, anyhow.

Just beyond Aspres-sur-Buech one comes to St.-Julien-en-Beauchêne, 100 kilometres from Digne. The Hôtel Bremond here is especially to be brought to the notice of the gastronome. It is a small and modest house, but the table is of the best and I can remember well eating there a very delicious ragoût, with mushrooms and a red wine sauce. At St.-Julien one is nearing the col and another quarter of an hour's run or so brings one over the pass. The run down from la Croix-Haute is magnificent. If one has not fed at St.-Julien, one can be well advised to stop at Monestier-de-Clermont, 50 kilometres further down.

The Hôtel de la Poste there is one of the most modest of houses. But do not be discouraged by its outward appearance. Within it is spotlessly clean and the cooking admirable. The lunch there costs (or cost) 13 francs only, and it is well worth the money. A little more than 30 kilometres further on brings one to Grenoble.

The traveller may, however, branch away to the

west, cutting out Grenoble, and coming into N.7, and the Rhône valley just below Valence. This, indeed, makes an agreeable alternative route, but not one to be advised in the winter season, the Col de Cabre (3870 feet) being apt to be blocked from time to time.

If the weather be suitable, and one chooses this road, one takes N.93 from Aspres-sur-Buech and can then stop for lunch (or dinner) and the night at le Luc-en-Diois. The Hôtel du Levant is the place to stop at. M. Curnonsky speaks of it as having 'the real cooking of France, simple and without "swank" (chichis), such as we love.' M. Curnonsky is certainly right. le Luc-en-Diois is 85 kilometres from Valence and 124 from Digne, making a convenient stepping-off place either way.

But to return to Grenoble.

In this city, I only know, personally, two restaurants. That of Philippe and that of the Trois Dauphins. I can heartily recommend the former. Of the Vautour, which M. Curnonsky and Rouff speak of as the most celebrated in Grenoble and which the 'Club-sans-Club' fails to mention, I know nothing. The Monnet Duglou, in the same square as the Philippe, also has a name, but I cannot speak of it from experience.

From Grenoble to what I suppose must be regarded as the incunabulum of French cooking is only 78 kilometres. I need hardly say that I speak of Belley – a town, in a literal sense, the incunabulum of Brillat-Savarin, who was born there on the 1st of April 1755. He died in Paris seventy-one years later; and thus, as his editor, M. Monselet, so succinctly puts it – 'he had time to eat.' One is also pleased to record and remember this fact against all the cranks and quacks who preach against good living. That one should eat and drink as well as Brillat-Savarin did and prolong his life to at least a year beyond the allotted span is an especially pleasant piece of evidence to conserve against miserable fanatics and unscrupulous scamps. And while one has arrived, as it were at Belley, the birthplace of Brillat-Savarin, it may be not irrelevant here to quote the twenty aphorisms of the Master. They are as apposite to-day as they were a century and more ago – and, perhaps, more needed. At least, their wisdom seems to have been largely forgotten by the modern world. They are as follows. I have endeavoured to translate them into their equivalent English, rather than adhere to a strict literalism.

The Axioms of Brillat-Savarin,

the which may alike serve as a Foreword to his work and as the fixed basis of the Science.

(1) The world is nought without life, and all that lives eats.
(2) Animals fill themselves: man eats; but it is the man of Intelligence alone who knows how to eat.
(3) The fate of Nations depends upon how they are fed.
(4) Tell me what you eat and I will tell you what you are.
(5) God, having made man to eat to live, has given him Appetite to tempt him and pleasure in satisfaction as its reward.

THE WINTER ROUTE

(6) Taste is the criterion of excellence.[1]
(7) The pleasures of the table are open to all — irrespective of age, class, country or time. They can be enjoyed together with other bodily delights and remain the last to console ourselves with when we have lost the others.
(8) At table is the one place where one is not bored — at least, for an hour.
(9) The discovery of a new dish does more for humanity than the discovery of a new planet.
(10) Gluttons and drunkards know neither how to eat nor drink.
(11) The right order of dishes is from the heavier to the lighter.
(12) The right order of drinks is from the lighter to the heavier.
(13) It is a mistake not to change the wine; for the palate becomes drugged and after the third glass, the best vintages will pall.
(14) Sweets without cheese are like a pretty woman with only one eye.
(15) One may be trained to the kitchen, but one must be born to the spit.
(16) The first quality in a cook is punctuality. It is not less so in a guest.
(17) To await, too long, a guest who is late, is but to insult those who are present.

[1] This aphorism reads as follows: 'La gourmandise est une acte de notre jugement, par lequel nous accordons la préférence aux choses qui sont agréables au goût sur celles qui n'ont pas cette qualité.'
It being impossible to translate 'gourmandise' into English, I have had to paraphrase very widely.

(18) He who is careless as to how he feeds his friends deserves to have none.

(19) It is the duty of the hostess to see to her coffee: of the host to see to his wines.

(20) To invite a guest is to debit yourself with his well-being the whole time he is under your roof.

Thus did the author of what we would, to-day, call The Psychology of Taste, lay down his epicurean principles. After a century and a half, the contemporary epicure will find but little to add thereunto; nor will he fail to find a kitchen at Belley worthy of such a place.

The traveller approaching this gastronomic altar from Grenoble, takes N.75, as far as les Abrets (46 kilometres), due care being taken to avoid the loop road to Voiron (viâ Moirans) – a mistake I have made myself more than once. From les Abrets, 32 kilometres along N.92 brings one to Belley. Of the town itself, I have not much to say. It seems to rain there more than any other place in France – at least, I have never had the good fortune to be there save in a torrential downpour.

The best-known hotel there is that, of course, of M. Pernolet, and his table is famous throughout France. His pastries filled with creamed écrevisse tails are beyond any praise – and I have eaten morilles there, also cooked in cream, such as I have encountered nowhere else. His chicken liver with truffles and mushrooms is a thing to dream of afterwards. Of the house itself – as I remember it in 1929 – I conserve the most pleasurable recollections. Of old-world rooms, and, much rarer, an old-world service, answering to the very touch of a bell. Of boiling water being brought into my bedroom in great copper cans and of a hot brick in a newspaper being placed under my feet, while I wrote a letter in the ante-room.

Alas, all this has now vanished, and I returned there last year to find the place being rebuilt and modernised according to the requirements of the Anglo-American tourist. Marble floors and porcelain basins: nickel-plated taps and private baths and all the paraphernalia of 'confort-moderne' were replacing wood floors and willing service and really hot water. Hot bricks had been supplanted by the work of the plumber. It may have been my fancy or not, but I did not find the cooking quite so good as it used to be in the modest, and no doubt less comfortable, past.

From Belley to Bourg is 75 kilometres. The first part of the road is not too easy to follow and I have twice gone wrong in it – once up and once down. One leaves Belley on G.C.31, and one can take two routes. The first is to follow G.C.31 as far as the hamlet of Pugieu, crossing the railway here into G.C.36, and so to Ambérieu; or one may take the first turning to the left off G.C. 31, about a kilometre outside Belley, into G.C.32, then on to G.C.41, picking up G.C.31, beyond Pugieu. This is, possibly, shorter in actual length, but it is a poor road. At Ambérieu, one cuts into N.75, 30 kilometres bringing one to Bourg. Bourg is famous for chickens and Matthew Arnold. I do not purpose to enlarge upon the Church of Brou here – you will find quite a lot about it in Baedeker – but for every hundred tourists who go to see this church scarcely one goes into the Church of Our Lady. If one delights at all in carving one should not fail to examine the choir stalls in Notre-Dame – preferably before the carving of your chicken – for the caricatures and grotesques there (one must turn up the seats and look underneath) are so vividly executed as to be more suitable for pre-prandial than post-prandial contemplation.

As to fowls and so forth, one can eat well almost anywhere in Bourg (an exception in cathedral towns) but my own choice is the Hôtel de l'Europe.

The kitchen of M. Rebière produces, in my opinion and experience, the best straight cooking in France – outside, possibly, Lyon and Paris. His full set meal, at 35 francs, is well worth the price. His specialities are as follows:

>Saucisson chaud
>Terrine de foies gras
>Quenelles truffées Nantua
>Volaille de Bresse à la crème
>Volaille gros sel
>Volaille de Bresse rôtie
>Truite de l'Ain
>Écrevisses du Pays

I can only add that the welcome and service in this admirable house are worthy of the excellence of the table. From Bourg to Chalon-sur-Saône is 81 kilometres, but I will leave the further detail of this journey northward for the following chapter.

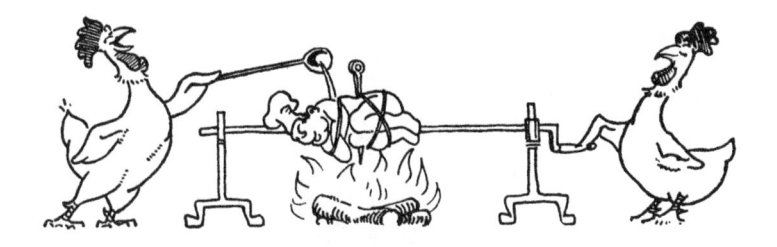

CHAPTER TEN

THE ALL-GOLD ROAD

IF you find yourself anywhere upon the fifth or sixth National Routes toward the end of January, moving northward, you will meet (and possibly be incommoded by) a stream of motor vehicles, for the most part luxurious and chauffeur-driven and also (for the most part) plastered on the back with a 'G.B.' These gentlemen – and ladies – are, of course, the great British Riviera public migrating southward for the seasonal splash at Monte Carlo, Cannes and Nice or hibernation at Menton, St.-Raphael or Hyères. Indeed, this particular route through Sens, Auxerre, Avallon, Saulieu and Chalon is very much the motoring equivalent of the Blue Train. The road is equipped with expensive hotels, specially designed to meet Anglican requirements. Chops and 'rosbif' decorate bills of fare: cocktails are ubiquitous; and even whiskies-and-soda grow like daisies at the roadside. Those indeed of a high index of insularity can, by a careful arrangement of their daily run, journey from Kensington to Cannes, without having to utter an un-English syllable; they

YOU CAN WEAR PLUS-FOURS ALL THE WAY DOWN

can comfortably remain, without exciting comment, in dinner-jackets and plus-fours all the way down and enjoy the genial atmosphere of the best West-end bars.

I do not propose to say much in these notes as to caravanserais of the class indicated above. The tourist agencies have a full list of them.

But although this road is, seasonally, so crowded with the nomadic rich as to be nicknamed the 'All-Gold,' good food and common civility may still be found upon it by the Ingenious Traveller; the more especially if he be able to time his journey outside the periods of influx into, and efflux out of, the Azure coast.

But he will scarcely find it, I fear, at Chalon-sur-Saône, the first town of importance to be reached from Mâcon or Bourg. At least, I have failed to find really agreeable entertainment in this town. The traveller will observe upon approaching the place, acres of posters advertising the merits of the Modern Hotel. I note that not only the 'Club-sans-Club,' but also M. Curnonsky, have much to say in favour of this hostelry. I have only entered the house once, but I then found the atmosphere of the place so displeasing that I had an apéritif only and dined in the town. Very likely I made a mistake, for I cannot find much to say for the Grand Café Brasserie, the which I chose on the strength of Michelin's two stars and the advice of a local inhabitant. The Hungry Traveller will be well advised to continue on for another 17 kilometres and eat and sleep at Chagny.

The house to go to at Chagny is the Hôtel du Commerce, an agreeable old house, pleasantly set in the centre square of the little town. M. Lameloise, the host, who is a lauréat of the T.C.F., will extend you the best of welcome and his cooking is of the first order. I ate an excellent little dinner there of, potage paysanne, brochet, and entrecôte, with salsify and salad, cheese and dessert – but the great delight of the evening was a bottle of Clos de Tart of '07 – the finest bottle of Burgundy I can remember to have drunk recently. M. Lameloise has also some admirable Marc.

If the Curious Traveller wishes to penetrate still further into the hinterland, he may be recommended to continue along N.6 for 11 kilometres from Chagny, and then take N.73 to the left to Nolay (4 kilometres). At Nolay – at the Hôtel Sainte-Marie – he will be well fed and wined, as well as comfortably housed in a modest style. I have dined and slept there, eating an admirably cooked meal of soup, brains, chicken and green peas, salad, asparagus, cheese and fruit. Needless to say, Nolay is well outside the provenance of the tourist, and its prices are as low as its entertainment is good. But to return to Chagny.

At Chagny, the north-bound traveller has two roads at his choice. He may branch to the right, taking N.74, through Beaune to Dijon, and from there on, either by N.5 to Sens, or by N.71 to Troyes. Or he may keep on directly on N.6, viâ Saulieu and Avallon.

We will suppose, first, that he takes the latter and more direct road. The 'spot' place to feed at on this road is, I imagine, Saulieu – at the Hôtel de la Poste. Although I have often had an apéro' there, en passant, I confess to having avoided eating within this well-known posting house. That it is as admirable as it is made out to be, I have no doubt; but some odd and egregious strain in me has so far deterred me from tasting of its delights. Perhaps I may be tempted so to do some day.

The Hungry Traveller, however, who is also modestly minded and content with simpler hospitality, may well be advised to lunch or dine at Arnay-le-Duc, a matter of some 30 kilometres south of Saulieu.

One should not be discouraged either by the outward appearance or the name of this little hotel – the Terminus. Hotels with such appellations – Terminus, de la Gare, etc., are, as a rule, to be avoided. The Terminus, at Arnay, is an illustrious exception to this rule; and the welcome and service there is as good as the food. One may note that so wide a traveller as Albert Londres has witnessed to the excellence of this house. I especially recommend the Thirsty Traveller to taste the Vieux Marc there: I have seldom, myself, tasted a better. The very clean (or, perhaps, the very dirty), who insist upon a bath had better go on to Saulieu.

From Saulieu to Avallon is another 38 kilometres, and at this latter place will be found one of the posting houses most dear to the Riviera motorist. In the migratory season the courtyard of this hotel will be found packed with Rolls-Royces as is a pod with peas. It is a very popular place with many people: and I was once induced to stop there the night. That was some little time ago now – but (as the song says) I don't suppose I'll do it again for years and years and years.

Before passing on to the Beaune-Dijon détour, it may be as well to consider an alternative road viâ

Autun, direct from Mâcon to Saulieu. To the lover of scenery this route is especially to be recommended.

On leaving Mâcon one takes N.79 for 19 kilometres, thence continuing on N.80, through Cluny, where the lace comes from. Some 80 kilometres more along N.80 brings one to Autun – where the buses stop.

For this reason, if for no other, the Gentle Traveller is advised to pass through Autun without more ado in the place than a modest apéritif. He can get cocktails (of a sort) at the Hôtel of St.-Louis and the Poste and drink them in a specially designed American bar, in the genial company of Motorways passengers – but if he be denationalised enough to enjoy a Byrrh, or a Pernod – a Picon or a St.-Raphael – I recommend the common café. Personally, I would push on (time allowing) to Saulieu.

If the Modest Traveller wishes a humble, but exceedingly good, entertainment, away altogether from the tourist traffic of the All-Gold Road, he cannot do better than continue on N.80 through Saulieu to Précy-sous-Thil. The little place is only 16 kilometres from Saulieu and at the Hôtel Terminus there the Humble Traveller will be well fed and watered – at a modest price – and escape the herd. I have had myself a memorable dinner there. One can also return into N.6 via N.70, cutting into the former, 20 kilometres north of Saulieu.

If the traveller wished to visit Dijon, he turns off N.6 (if moving northward), just beyond Chagny, to the right into N.74, reaching Beaune in 16 kilometres.

He is here at the G.H.Q. of the Burgundy industry, and at the famous Hôtel de la Poste he can taste as many vintages as his purse may allow. I suppose it is really very wonderful (it is some years since I last lunched there) since the 'Club-sans-Club' (1930) tells you to count upon 85 francs for 'un repas très soigné.' I am afraid I forget what my meal cost me then in '27 – as also what I ate. . . .

A short run from Beaune brings one to Dijon – a town famous (amongst other things) for mustard. I can thoroughly recommend the mustard – more particularly, the Grey-Poupon. For the rest, there are several monuments with which this work is not concerned. Burgundy, of course, can be drunk there, as at Beaune. There is a very large hotel, much favoured by English and Americans, which possesses very large and luxurious rooms with prices in harmony and a kitchen appropriate to its clientèle. The welcome is what one would expect in a railway station: so is the service. I only know one other hotel in Dijon, the which I liked even less than the former. The few times I have been to Dijon, I fear I have been foolish enough to have chosen (and paid for) luxury at the expense of *gemüthlichkeit*. That there are other small, comfortable and moderate hotels in Dijon (many French people go there) I feel sure. Some day I must try to find one.

Of restaurants in Dijon, the Trois Faisans is the most famous. I have eaten many a good meal there and drank fine Burgundy. No one in his senses would suggest that the cooking at the Trois Faisans is anything but of the best; yet, although I have lunched or dined there a number of times, it is by no means a house that has especially appealed to me. It is hard to explain, in any exact sense, anything lacking. The

A WELCOME AS IN A RAILWAY STATION

cellar, of course, is admirable, the bill of fare varied and elegant, the quality of the cooking without reproach, the service assiduous, and yet. . . . I don't know? One could name half a dozen better houses in Lyon; but it is scarcely fair to compare any other town to Lyon. I think the truth of the matter really is that the Three Pheasants tends to suffer a little from its reputation. The place is so talked about that one looks for more than one really has a right to expect. . . .

Of other restaurants in Dijon (Palace Hotel dining-rooms can, of course, be ignored) I only know the Châteaubriand. I ate one of the best pig's trotters there I have ever eaten in my life, and the prices were moderate – so was the service: so moderate, that you would be lucky to get anything to eat at all. If you don't mind waiting an hour for your food and then having it thrown at your head when you get it, the Châteaubriand gives fair value for the money. I am told, on good authority, that the station Buffet is excellent. Next time I feed in Dijon, I intend to try it.

From Dijon, the northward traveller has two main routes open to him. He may strike more directly northward through Châtillon-sur-Seine to Troyes and Soissons, leaving Paris on the left. This road will be considered in the next chapter. Or, if he wishes to make for Paris, he will take N.5, to Tonnerre and Sens. Should he, however, care to make a small détour so as to cut into N.6 at Arnay-le-Duc, and see a very lovely bit of country, he should turn off N.5, at Sombernon, into N.77 bis. If he does this, he will pass through the tiny hamlet of Comarin ($7\frac{1}{2}$ kilometres from Sombernon) and catch a glimpse of one of the most delightful and unspoilt châteaux in this part of France. la Rochepot, below Arnay, is more imposing and better placed, but the restoration has, to my mind, destroyed much of its charm.

To revert back again to the All-Gold Road, from Avallon to Auxerre is only some 50 kilometres. Just before coming to Arcy-sur-Lure upon this road one tunnels under a curious rock formation. Near here are famous prehistoric caves. At Auxerre, the Hungry Traveller can be well cared for at the Touring or at the Epée. Both hotels are under the same administration, and there is little to choose between them. Some years ago the table at the Epée was excellent, but there has, to my mind, been a sad falling off in latter years, owing no doubt to the vast increase in the British motor traffic and the growing popularity of Auxerre as a stepping-off place among this public. The last time I dined at the Touring, the company in the dining-room was, without exception, English or American and the menu in accordance with the guests.

From Auxerre to Sens is scarcely more than an hour's run. In the latter place, the presence of so well-known a monument as its cathedral has not swept the town of possible places at which to eat. At least, it had not the last time I lunched there.

Of the Hôtel de Paris there, I can speak with the highest praise and the deepest affection. Of its type, I scarcely know a better house in France. It is of the old-fashioned kind, visited by commercial gentlemen who sit at a centre table and offering to its guests three set meals, priced at 18, 25, and 35 francs. It is that solid and reputable kind of house, where one washes one's hands outside in the passage at a single tap – drying them on a roller towel. In such houses, one always feels safe as to the cooking. But all this may well be changed by now. It is two years since I dined there. A great deal may happen in two years. If once the proprietor gets the idea of an English clientèle and plunges into sanitary excesses and the like and sticks up an AA or an R.A.C. over his door, all will be lost. And that reminds me. The epicure travelling in France must remember never, never, never to stop at an inn flaunting either of these heraldic signs. For reasons not far to seek, these decorations are death warrants to the culinary art in France. Though, of course, there is always the exception to prove the rule.

The traveller from the Morvan may (or may not) wish to stop at Fontainebleau – a town of historic interest, chiefly composed of hotels. The most elaborate hotel (at least in the town) is that of France and England, situated opposite the Palace. It is an interesting house; and if you wish to sleep in 'period' rooms (at a price), by all means sleep there. The set dinner (or lunch) costs 60 francs: if you order à la carte you can pay very much more. The house has a really marvellous collection of coloured prints, cartoons and caricatures the which it is well worth while to go in and see at whatever the maître d'hôtel considers you will pay for a cocktail. The more entertaining examples are discreetly relegated to the gentlemen's cloak-room.

The question of prices – so instant with all but the millionaire traveller – is an interesting analysis: in particular, as to how Anglo-Saxon tourism has affected them. The following table is illuminating:

124 THE HUNGRY TRAVELLER IN FRANCE

PLACE.	HOTEL.	PRICE OF DINNER.		
		Baedeker 1905.	Michelin 1930.	Multiple increase.
(A).—Towns affected by the English.				
Fontainebleau	France et Angleterre	5	60	12 times
Rouen	de la Poste	3.5	35	10 ,,
Avallon	de la Poste	3	30	10 ,,
Auxerre	Épée	3	32	10.7 ,,
Autun	de la Poste	3.5	35	10 ,,
Mont St.-Michel	Rest. Poulard	3	32	10.7 ,,
Caen	Angleterre	4	35	8.7 ,,
Le Mans	Dauphin	3.5	30	8.6 ,,
Tours	Univers	5	40	8 ,,

Average increase, 9.7.

(B).—Towns unaffected by the English.

Epinal	(First hotel)	3.5	15	4.3 times
Laval	Paris (starred in Michelin)	3	18	6 ,,
Rennes	France	4	18	4.5 ,,
Vire	Cheval Blanc (starred in Michelin)	3	15	5 ,,
Gien	de la Poste	3	16	5.3 ,,

Average increase, 5.

It will be seen from these few places, chosen at random in the north of France, how the effect of Anglo-Saxon tourism has raised prices. As the quality of the table invariably deteriorates when Britons sit at it, it is not to be surprised that such French as travel (and all gourmets) dread the approach of the English as they would a blight. It may be pointed out in respect to the above examples, that the actual average percentage rise in really small places (of which Baedeker gives no figures) between 1905 and 1930 is, in reality, well under the 5 index figure quoted above. One may take it that the cost of travelling in France should not be more than it was before the War in reference to a gold standard – which represents an average multiple of 5. The multiple cost index of 'luxuries' in France to-day as compared to that prevalent just before the War, is very probably equal to the gold exchange value – namely about 5. When I was a student at Montpellier in 1913, we used to buy a sound bottle of champagne of a known house (Mumm, Moët, Lanson, etc.) for 5 francs. The local retailer now sells the same thing for 25 francs. The cost ratio of necessities is, of course, lower. Wherever the gilded Nordic disports himself the multiple index rises easily to 10 or more; and fantastic figures can be reported to the credit of his polymorphic soul. I remember visiting last year a miserable mud-bank, plastered with jerry-built villas, where I had to pay 225 francs a night for a single room only (3rd floor) at the principal hotel of the place – out of season. Needless to say, it is a resort (not Deauville) entirely given over to the English and the American. Considering anyone can get a double room and bath of his choice at the best hotels at Cannes, Nice or Monte Carlo (out of season) for never more than 120 francs – I insist usually on 80 – the folly of paying such prices is apparent. I see from my 1905 Baedeker that, at that time, the one hotel in the place charged about 5 francs a night for a room. An increase of at least 4500 per cent. in letable value says something for the promoters of the place.

One can, however – or, at least, one could two years ago – feed well at Fontainebleau without pouring money into the maw of Limited Liability Companies. I refer to the Pavillon Bleu, in the Boulevard Magenta. The last time I lunched there, I was saddened to hear that the proprietor was quitting his pleasant pavilion and garden to open a more luxurious establishment elsewhere. I well remembering eating, at the old Blue Pavilion, a Châteaubriand of an exquisite tenderness, rare to find in France; as, also, the best morilles I have ever tasted anywhere. I sincerely hope, in the future, the new cuisine will not be made to pay for what the French so happily nominate as 'cadre.' I, personally, would rather eat a good mushroom in a cellar than a bad mushroom in a cathedral; the former is more pleasurable at the time and (possibly) less tiresome afterwards.

But, then, of course, I am a pig!

CHAPTER ELEVEN

THROUGH THE WAR ZONE

From Dijon to Troyes – a matter of some 150 kilometres – makes a very pleasant morning's run; but one should start in good time so as to reach Troyes before midday. For Troyes is proud in possessing one of the first altars to gastronomy in all France; and the epicure will need to spend at least two hours over his lunch there. In fact, in the limits of my own experience, I consider Troyes as ranking in the first five eating places outside the capitals: namely with Cap Ferrat, Poitiers, Beauvais and Vienne (vide supra).

The Hungry Traveller must not be discouraged because this altar is raised in a railway station. One can sit at table at this Buffet and watch, through the window, the trains come and go and hear (indistinctly) the loud speaker announcing their movements. But these are the only indications that one is in a station restaurant – for the kitchen, the cellar and the service would do credit to the famous houses of Lyon, Marseille or Bordeaux.

The motorist, arriving in Troyes and wishing to eat at the Buffet, may conveniently drive into the garage of the Grand Hôtel, where he will leave his car and from there climb up and into the house. He will pass through this house – a comfortable one, thoroughly modernised with a dance hall and an American bar – where he may drink if necessary – and thence pass down and out again into the station yard and to the Buffet. There is not (as far as I am aware) a dining-room in the hotel.

Baedeker starred this station Buffet more than a quarter of a century ago; and goes on to say, rather unkindly, that Troyes was once a place of great commercial importance, but is now chiefly celebrated for hosiery and pork. Michelin is kinder and more specific, citing, as well as hosiery, pork sausages and snails.

The last time I ate at Troyes, I devoured none of these – because, in the first place, I am not over fond of andouillettes, however well made, and in the second, snails, then, were out of season. I ate, instead, a simple, but perfectly cooked and ordered meal as follows:

> Hors-d'œuvres
> Pâtés Maison variés
> Sole Meunière
> Perdreau sur Canapé
> Pomme Paille
> Fromage
> Fruits

It has always been an axiom of mine that hors-d'œuvres variés are the supreme test of a meal. If these are good, you need have no fear of what follows. It is – I will not say always, but almost always – the acid test of a good dinner. Many a tale begins well and ends badly – many an author can intrigue you with a prelude and weary you with a play; but few cooks succeed in the hors and fail in the chefs-d'œuvres; perhaps because the former are more difficult to make.

If the traveller, when he reaches Troyes, wishes to turn eastward into Germany, he can very conveniently do so from this city, by taking N.60 viâ Nancy to Strasbourg. As I have already noted, N.60 between Troyes and Joinville, was in a shocking state the last time I was on it. It may be mended by now.

Of Nancy, I know nothing except by report and that was unfavourable to epicurean entertainment in this town. When using the 60th national, I stopped myself (for dinner and the night) at Joinville, in the Haute Marne, 93 kilometres east of Troyes. I can thoroughly recommend the Gentle and the Hungry Traveller to do the same. The Hôtel de la Poste there is a small and modest house – but the accommodation is clean and comfortable and the table excellent. The welcome is cordial and the charges remarkably low. It is better to avoid stopping there on a Sunday, as the dining-room is then apt to be overcrowded.

At Strasbourg (where the foie gras comes from) the Hungry Traveller need not be afraid of starving. Strasbourg is, indeed, worthy to be numbered as one of the four capitals of gastronomy outside Paris – and M. Zimmer, as one of the best cooks in France.

I feel a very particular affection for M. Zimmer, personally; for when, two years ago, I was alone in

I

Strasbourg and used to dine nightly at his table, he treated me more as a guest than as a client; inviting me to drink with him bottles of old wine, not listed to his public, and to eat, from time to time, at his own table. He was quite the most genial and generous host I have ever met anywhere. You will find the best pâté in the world at Zimmer's: especially, I recommend the epicure to taste it fresh – as a hot dish. But this should be eaten in moderation: it is about the richest thing in food there is. M. Zimmer has also some notable Alsace wines, as well as admirable old Quèstch. Quite a good meal is served at the Maison Rouge – the best (and most expensive) hotel in the town; but I have a poor opinion of Valentine Sorg – whose reputation is so wide. I do not say that the cooking is bad, but the service is so perfunctory that no epicure of Taste and Judgment would expose himself twice to such treatment. Perhaps the service has improved since last I was there; I sincerely hope so for the sake of a house that has (or had) a great name.

The traveller wishing to make a circular tour to Strasbourg and back, may well plan his return journey, either across the Vosges to Dijon or through Franche-Comté to Besançon and the south. The latter route, unless one especially wishes to see the district, I do not recommend. The roads are (or, at least, were) what the French would call 'quelconque' and Besançon is – in my opinion – one of the dullest towns in France. As the very home and temple of the small rentier and of the impecunious retired, this, perhaps, is not to be wondered at: one scarcely expects a hectic gaiety in a Tunbridge Wells, whose inhabitants subsist on rents paid in a currency inflated five times. I once spent a night there and dined at the Casino: I do not propose to do either the one or the other again.

The alternative route across the Vosges is a very lovely one, particularly the road between Munster and Remiremont, where one passes the lakes of Longemer and Gerardmer. The Epicurean Traveller taking this road is particularly urged not to stop at Colmar – a place somewhat overburdened with the military – but to go out to Kaysersberg, some 10 kilometres away to the west. This delightful and picturesque little place is not only notable as being one of the very few towns in France beginning with a K, but also for the Hôtel Chambard, whose table and cellar are a real delight. One is especially advised to eat the truite bleu and drink the Riquewihr there.

As to eating and drinking in the Vosges, I know next to nothing. I lunched when crossing them, at Luxeuil, where I had an exceedingly poor meal thrown at me in what I supposed to be the best hotel. The place, altogether, seemed to me to be most inappropriately named.

If one decides to strike northward from Troyes, I can do no better than advise the gourmet to make it an afternoon's run to Soissons – a matter of 150 kilometres. This town, of course, was practically destroyed in the late War, and the main street presents the odd appearance of the stage of a theatre. The houses are, so to speak, only skin deep; and a peep down every side street discloses ruins and rubble heaps. But at the Croix d'Or, one can eat well and sleep in luxury. This – a well-known house in the past – has, of course, been entirely rebuilt in the modern manner; but here (unlike in so many houses) comfort and decorations have not ruined the kitchen, the cellar or the service – all of which deserve the highest commendation.

Should one wish to visit Reims, about an hour's run from Soissons along N.31 brings one to it. If you like gloating over war ruins, by all means go there. Otherwise, the town has been vilely and hideously rebuilt. I am told it is peculiarly a 'red' town, and from the lack of common civility to visitors I am ready to believe it is. I both dined and slept there at a cost in inverse ratio to the board and lodging. No doubt the hosts of English and Americans who go there to see the battlefields and swill champagne has debauched the hôtellerie. Should one move directly northward, 123 kilometres from Soissons brings one to Arras. It is, of necessity, a dreary road, following as it does, the battle line all the way. At Arras, I was lucky enough to fall upon my feet in respect to food. There is a new and elaborate barrack of a hotel which may or may not have a kitchen, but I had the good sense to stop a man in the street and ask his advice about the matter. He very earnestly recommended a more modest establishment – the Hôtel du Petit St.-Eloi, in the rue Briquet-Taillandier. M. Boulissière there is a chef of the first quality. I ate one of the best Châteaubriand, with pomme paille, I have enjoyed recently. The set meal is an extended one and the price amazingly reasonable. I may also add that one can buy there a bottle of Burgundy at a moderate price and of the highest quality. A happy combination of events, as rare to find in Burgundy as elsewhere.

I should like to add that the unknown gentleman

who directed me to this delightful little eating-house (to which he was accustomed to go himself) was not a native of Arras, but a 'mutilé' of the War, who had to come to Arras as his centre, to collect his pension. If you happen to know (*a*) what a real Frenchman – pas de métèques – considers food, and (*b*) what a man who has lost an arm is paid, in France, for the loss of it, and (*c*) what stipend an employee in the prefecture – (anglicé, clerk to the urban district council) is likely to receive, you will realise that I have seldom eaten a better meal at a lower cost. . . . Hélas! Most of us to-day, of an age to take pleasure in the palate, can but remember with regret how little those delights cost us when we were too young to enjoy them.

Ego et in arcadia vixi, may well be the motto of the contemporary Epicurean. For however sad a dog one may have been, few of us to-day are what the Italians so happily call 'pescicani,' dog-fish or profiteers. If I speak, and have spoken, too much of money, it is to be remembered that the irony of the Aristippian heresy to-day is that the moneyed cannot understand and the understanding cannot pay.

THIRD JOURNEY – ACROSS

CHAPTER TWELVE

THE VAR

The department of the Var, of which Draguignan is the capital, is one of the largest in France. It stretches nearly as far as Cannes in the east and to la Ciotat in the west. Its northern border follows the Cañon of the Verdon, but just missing Castellane. There is (with the possible exceptions of the Alpes-Maritimes and Basses-Pyrénées) no department in all France so given over to the English as is the Var. This is particularly so in respect to the resident – as apart from the tourist of the hotels – be he but the monthly tenant of a furnished flat or the more full-blooded lessee, liable to income-tax. The piece of coast, for example, between la Napoule and St.-Tropez – of which St.-Raphael is the glittering capital – is almost entirely inhabited by English residents. The strip beyond St.-Tropez, towards Hyères, is more the appanage of the French middle-class than of the English, but at Hyères the former come into their own again with tea and golf. Toulon itself is fairly free from Britannic occupation, being the most anti-English town in France: partly because of Nelson and partly because the Orient boats disgorge our Empire-builders there once a week. Bandol and Cassis, further west, are, however, great strongholds of the English settler, and the rapidly growing 'bungalow town' of les Lèques will probably soon rival both.

It might be imagined that in this almost denationalised department – with Tooting and the Thames valley spread out up and down the coast – there would be little of interest to be found even by the most curious of epicures. And, indeed, as far as concerns those districts taken over by the English colonists, this is very true. I remember once – and once only, I am thankful to say – being obliged, owing to misbehaviour on the part of my car – to spend a night at St.-Raphael. I remember it well, for it was Christmas Eve; and I ate one of the worst meals I have ever eaten in recent years, in one of the first hotels there, in an exclusively English company, where I was conspicuous in a lounge suit. I can even remember the menu – which was much as follows:

> Soup (made with squares)
> An anonymous white fish (demi-froid)
> Mutton cutlets, with beans (the stringy sort)
> Leg of a chicken and mashed potatoes
> Caramel cream
> Cheese
> Fruit

The bananas were quite good; otherwise the meal was somewhat of a failure.

But the English – the English colonists even – are

happily rather like the rind of a cheese – they form but a narrow strip along the coast line; and gastronomic adventure of a high order may be found in the Var, nine-tenths of which is still unexplored by hotel companies and estate agencies. From the point of view of the gourmet, the most entertaining town in the Var, is, no doubt, its one-time capital Toulon. It is not, to be sure, a town notable for its hotels: although one can even get comfortable accommodation there at a reasonable price. In this respect, I can personally recommend the Hotel Victoria. But it boasts one quite good restaurant and a cook, who is unrivalled, even in Marseille. The former is the Au Sourd. I have known this restaurant for some seven years, and although it has changed its management (at least once) in this period, I have found its excellence unimpaired and (I might add) its errors uncorrected. To speak of this small matter first, the Au Sourd boasts one of the slowest services in the south of France – which is saying a great deal. I do not mean that the service is bad – the manners of the staff are most courteous – but it is slow; and I mention this the more particularly so as to warn the epicure to order his meal well beforehand. If you do this and take some trouble in your choice and are decently civil to the maître d'hôtel, you will not fail to eat there an elegant meal. But it is not the slightest use going into the Au Sourd with the manners of a drill-sergeant. You'll be lucky if you get anything to eat at all. Your Provençal is not a man to be hurried, and the Au Sourd regards itself as a very quiet and serious eating-house and not an American quick-lunch counter. Also, do not go there – in fact get out of Toulon altogether, if you can – the day the boat comes in. On such days, even this humble restaurant is often discovered by the Orientals – if one may so nominate them – and on such occasion the staff there acts the proverbial puppy and lies on its back with all four paws in the air! Even putting money on its paws doesn't make it stand up – and having watched for years the comedy of 'gentlemen of England, cleanly-bred and machinely-crammed' being unloaded in Toulon – I cannot say that I blame them.

But in between boat times one fares there very well indeed. I can recommend the bouillabaisse, but remember that this is a dish which requires a special variety of fish, which may or may not be at the moment available. Also, if you ask for it in the evening you will probably be laughed at. If you like garlic, try the tomates provençal. In season, the Au Sourd is good with game – particularly with grives – and their langouste à l'Armoricaine is admirable. I can speak well of the Château Grillet.

I spoke, a little way back, of a cook in Toulon. There is, indeed, one there worthy to be addressed as Maître. He is one of the best cooks in Provence and one of the shyest. His eating-house is not easy to find. It took me two years to discover it myself. For this artist displays no sign or advertisement to inform the passer-by where he may so delicately eat. His restaurant, indeed, consists but of three small rooms above a chemist's shop – one of which is the kitchen.

It is not advisable to go in there without previously warning the Master of your intention. He more or less cooks to order, and you may (if you chance it) do no more than pick up the crumbs from an epicurean's table. No: go and see the Master a good two hours before lunch (better still, the day before) and arrange with him for your meal. His is the master hand for bouillabaisse – even rivalling Marseille, and he can roast a partridge to the divided second of perfection. He is, I believe, a retired Navy cook. By the way, I should warn the epicure that he is a man of character, like any great artist, and requires careful handling. It is better to let him design your meal for you – at least, if you do not, you are scarcely likely to get it. I may add that, despite the Anglo-Saxon colonisation of the Var, I have never seen an Englishman at his table; and, indeed, I fancy I owe my own immunity there to the good services of the Baron de B—, who vouched for me. Now it only remains for me to give the name of this master cook of cooks and the exact indication of the house in which he practises his art – and I intend to do neither. It were but a poor return for such perfect entertainment, to broadcast its address and so loose upon it the ravening hordes of tourism. It would be an ill service to the good Toulonnais himself, who finds it no easy matter to eat anywhere, finely and modestly, untroubled by 'ces barbares, les Anglais,' with more money than manners and more talk than taste – such as the Parisian, tormented in the same way, so aptly describes as 'punaises' – because you can't get rid of them!

No: nor would it even help the Traveller of Taste and Discretion so to do. For, in a year, the place would have vanished – or else, blossomed out into a restaurant de luxe with a bar and a jazz-band and a kitchen appropriate to this aesthetic. I have given an indication: it is enough. The Englishman, not too insular, with a tongue in his head and ability to use it, will be able to find the place for himself. Having done so, he will not be likely to disclose it to any but the dilettante and the discreet.

In summer-time, however, one may wish to lunch or dine outside the town: if possible, on the coast, where one may enjoy the sea air – and the mosquitoes. For such desiderata – as also for good food – one can scarcely do better than go to Père Louis, on the other side of the Rade.

This old and reputed restaurant is most pleasantly situated on a slight slope overlooking the harbour of Toulon. It is actually in Balaguier, an outlying district of la Seyne. By road, one has to follow the tram lines to la Seyne all round the harbour, but an almost quicker way is to take the steamer (every few minutes) across to la Seyne and walk from there. I know few things pleasanter than, on a warm summer's evening, to dine there, on the wide terrace, and watch the lights come out, one by one, over all the waters of the Rade. You should order your dinner beforehand. The house has been famous for over a century and it had, a few years ago, some wonderful Napoléon brandy of which I am glad to say, I bought up the last seven bottles. But the intending diner need not be discouraged: I feel sure some more has been made by now.

I said just now that the service at the Au Sourd was the slowest in Provence. I am wrong. Père Louis can beat the Au Sourd by a good half-hour. He has two charming daughters who wait – but nothing like so long as the guests do. None the less, the food is admirable and the place delightful; and, after all, why be in a hurry in Provence in the summer-time – or any other time as far as that goes? It's no good, anyhow, since you won't get anywhere if you are. The only time a true Provençal is ever seen to hurry is to get inside his house when the mistral begins to blow – where he remains in bed for the requisite three, six or nine days until it is over.

I might add the usual caveat as to not going there on a Sunday, unless you wish to observe the local dockyard contractor and the like in gala mood. It is, believe me, an interesting study, but one more suitable to the sociologist than the epicurean.

If the Curious Traveller wishes to explore, in a gastronomic sense, the remoter recesses of local life round and about Toulon, he can be well advised to visit les Pins-de-Galles. This can only be done in summer, nor is it – as it sounds – a misprint for the Prince of Wales. This remote settlement of summering shopkeepers is by no means as Anglophile as that, but why the Mediterranean pines among which these shacks are sheltered should be especially dedicated to Wales is a crux I have been unable to elucidate.

It is, in every sense of the word, an odd place. How to get there is not easy to explain. One takes the road to that suburb of Toulon called le Mourillon – the which one leaves on the right – and continues further eastward for about a kilometre, then takes a narrow by-road to the right, leading to the coast. This road is a cul-de-sac. One leaves the car there – at the top of the cliff – and scrambles down through a Peter Panish

A PROVENÇAL WORKER

village among the pine trees, to the beach – above which, on a few rough planks – is the restaurant.

If you want to eat really fresh grilled crayfish – straight out of the sea – or whatever else may be available at the time of sea-fruit – this is the place to come to. It is a typical casse-croûte and one eats off bare boards. Also, it is advisable not only to warn the fisherfolk beforehand of your coming, but also to bring your own bread, butter and wine with you. I know no other place in the south where you can get such fish and so cooked; but it is to be eaten at a fisherman's table, and I warn the traveller who is too dainty to mix with his betters, and/or unable to speak their language, to abandon any attempt to seek entertainment among the Welsh pines.

As to Sundays and Holy Days, the same remarks apply to the Pins-des-Galles as to all gastronomic temples within easy distance of a busy town. I might add that the bathing here is altogether delightful. The sand, the scenery and the rocks are far finer than, for example, Juan-les-Pins and (Sundays, etc., excepted) there is much more room in the sea; and you can eat your langouste in your bathing-dress – if you like – afterwards, at a hundredth of the cost. I am afraid that it will not be reported in the Daily Press that you have done these exciting things – but you cannot expect everything for nothing. There is no Casino at les Pins-de-Galles, but no one will stop you playing shove-halfpenny on the table afterwards, if you want to. Certainly not the policeman, for the simple – but quite adequate reason – that no policeman has probably ever been there.

The traveller, wishing to see something of the hinterland and not starve in doing it, may well be advised to seek out Montreuil-le-Vieux. This charming spot can be very comfortably visited by the west-bound traveller upon N.7, from Brignoles.

In this case, he follows N.7, for 5 kilometres to the west of Brignoles and then turns south into G.C.105 – following this road, through Roquebrusanne as far as Méounes, 22 kilometres from Brignoles. There is an admirable eating-house at Méounes – namely the inn of M. Trottobas – peculiarly noted for écrevisse and game.

To visit Montreuil-le-Vieux, one passes through Méounes, and takes the first turning to the right after leaving the village – that is G.C.105A. About five minutes' run along this brings one to the lane leading, across the stream, to the restaurant – and one-time monastery – beautifully set upon the ruins of the older building and flanked by its large gardens, irrigated by streams and backed by the forest. One should go there in summer-time, so as to eat in the garden. The cooking is excellent and their specialities are trout, écrevisse and game. The usual warning as to Sunday and fête days applies, of course, both to here and to Méounes. From Montreuil, one may continue along G.C.105A to Signes and from there on G.C.124, until one strikes N.8, at le Camp. Thirty-six kilometres brings one into Marseille. Just beyond Signes, one climbs up the gorge of the Gapeau and, if the river is in spate, it is worth while to stop there a moment to look at the waterfall.

If one wishes, however, to turn south to Toulon, G.C.105A must be retraced into G.C.105 and this latter road followed south until it cuts into the 97th National at Solliès-Pont – 14 kilometres from Toulon.

From Toulon to Marseille, two routes are open to the traveller – the coast road and the inland road. By the former, one passes through la Seyne, Sanary, Bandol, la Ciotat and Cassis: by the latter, through Ollioules (and its gorge) le Bausset, Cuges, and Aubagne. This latter is the better and shorter road. At Aubagne, however, one picks up that peculiar bane to the motorist – namely, the tram-lines – which one has to endure for the last 17 kilometres of the journey. By the coast road, one suffers only a few kilometres of these nuisances.

If one chooses the coast road, one should arrange to lunch at Sanary – for it is in this pleasant little fishing village that the great Hiély himself has taken up his retreat. I find myself unable to speak too highly of the pleasant little hotel and restaurant that M. and Mme Hiély have here in Sanary. They are, themselves, the most perfect of hosts, and their table admirable. There is a set meal at 16 francs, worth double the price. But to enjoy to the full M. Hiély's great art, one should consult him the day before. His langouste à l'Armoricaine is a marvel, as also his grilled loup or dorade, and (as I have already mentioned) he can cook a grive à la Provençal as no one else can. This dish which is a thrush cooked en casserole, with black olives and whole garlics, is not commonly known to English people (who generally are prejudiced against garlic) but it is, none the less, when well done, a veritable poem of a dish. Another local dish to be noted are squids. Badly cooked, these small octopi are apt to be suggestive of

K

the best india-rubber: but well-cooked they are a dream — transcending in delicacy (to my mind) even the oyster. But the would-be eater of them is not advised to see them caught – a somewhat unpleasant sight, as they are hooked up out of the rocks on the end of a long cane and quickly turned inside out to render them innocuous. I once saw a Provençal fisherman – faced with a peculiarly large and tough squid – hold the animal with both hands, while he pulled it inside out with his teeth. ... No; squid-catching is not a sport to be recommended to the squeamish.

From Sanary one follows G.C.16, through Bandol. I have eaten there a number of times very dismally, and I do not suggest that the Gentle Traveller stop there at all – unless he has a fancy for imbibing whiskies and soda to the accompaniment of a gramophone and epicene back-chat – but then, of course, he would cease to be gentle. Nor do I advise his lunching at the next place, les Lèques, unless he wishes to study – at close quarters – a number of stupid young suburbans – and some stupid old ones – being what they think is naughty.

Leaving les Lèques, one skirts la Ciotat (where the Messageries Maritimes has its dockyards) and strikes inland, turning to the left to Cassis, when one has climbed up to the col. One can eat well enough there, but it is sadly given over to the English squatter – of the Bohemian, or would-be Bohemian variety.

The run from Cassis into Marseille on G.C.1 is marvellously picturesque and affords the finest panorama of Marseille and its harbour, but the road is narrow, winding and steep and its surface is (or was) abominable. It is not to be recommended to the inexpert driver or the under-powered car. If the inland road (N.8) be followed a word should be said as to the propriety of stopping for a meal at the Villa Venuse at Gemenos. Gemenos itself is actually off the Marseille Road. At Coulin (travelling westward) one takes the right branch (N.96 – as though going to Aix) but turns off to the right after $2\frac{1}{2}$ kilometres into G.C.2. The Restaurant Venuse is on the left of the road.

The table here is excellent and one can eat in a pleasantly shaded garden. It has – or had – a well-stocked cellar, and I remember eating a poulet cocotte there of exceptional delicacy.

Should one have time to spare and wish to visit one of the most remarkable view-points in this district, one may continue along G.C.2 until one comes to the Hôtellerie de la Ste.-Baume – a matter of some 23 kilometres from Gemenos, but a narrow and winding road. The order that occupy the monastery here give entertainment to visitors – not luxurious, as is to be supposed – but good, clean and cheap. The ascent of St.-Pilon – which begins just at the back of the monastery – takes about an hour. The highest point – on which is set a pilgrimage chapel – reaches some 3200 feet. The panorama is magnificent. By continuing on along I.C.38 past the Hôtellerie one can reach the Seventh National at St.-Maximin, 19 kilometres from Brignoles.

Gemenos, by the way, as also Cassis and la Ciotat, is beyond the border of the Var: Ste.-Baume is just within it.

CHAPTER THIRTEEN

FROM SEA TO SEA

Leaving Marseille to be dealt with in a chapter to itself later, I will suppose the traveller, still reasonably hungry, to be trekking from this city across the peninsula to Bordeaux. The first lap on this route will take him inevitably through Salon and Arles, to Nîmes, and the first place of any importance that he comes to, after leaving Marseille, is Salon – a run of 49 kilometres on an excellent road, once one has escaped from the purlieus of Marseille. Salon is an agreeable, old-world town, chiefly noted for the richness of its inhabitants – who are, so to speak, all olive-oil millionaires. Indeed, it boasts a club in the middle of the town, almost approaching the English standard in appearance, the which one must not mistake for the hotel, as I did, the last time I was there. As to hotels, I doubt if one can do better than to feed at the Angleterre, which is next door to the aforesaid club. The food there is varied and well cooked, the price modest, and the welcome cordial.

The road to Salon, by the way, skirts a portion of the famous salt-water lake known as the Étang de Berre, nearly a hundred square miles in area. If one wishes to visit Martigues, situated on the southern edge of the Étang, and named, or misnamed, the Provençal Venice, one takes the left-hand fork at les Pennes, into G.C.14: 22 kilometres from the fork brings one to Martigues.

Martigues — which Baedeker very properly describes as a decayed town — is the dirtiest place I know of in the south of France, and is chiefly composed of smells, flies, jelly-fish and landscape painters. The jelly-fish are the most interesting of the four. I have never seen such large ones and so many anywhere else; and when they get stranded on the foreshore and decay in the sun, one understands the smells of the place and becomes more charitable to the artists. I only stopped there some seven hours — it was quite long enough — and lunched at the local hotel with a few thousand flies. I think the Delicate Traveller will continue on to Salon direct, and leave the Provençal Venice to be Venetian all by itself.

From Salon to Arles is 40 kilometres. This road — G.C.4 — crosses the Crau, an absolutely flat plain, covered with small round pebbles and swept, with terrific force, by the mistral. The first 29 kilometres of this road is absolutely straight, absolutely flat and entirely devoid of trees or houses either side. The road is wide, and the motorist who wishes to attempt a speed record could scarcely find a better stretch of road in al France. Provided, of course, that the mistral is not blowing — in which event he may find himself ditched at any speed over sixty miles an hour. To the left of this road, some 12 kilometres to the south, is the famous racing track of Miramas. There is not much to be found of an edible nature between Salon and Arles unless the Hungry Traveller can digest stones. At Arles there are hotels – as well as an amphitheatre. This town, indeed, used to be famous for two hotels, both under the same management, so that the small square of the Forum used to exhibit the entertaining sight of visitors, dissatisfied with the hospitality of the Forum Hotel, streaming across to the Nord, and those dissatisfied with the Nord, streaming across to the Forum, without any sensible injury to the owners of the two principal hotels in the town. Since then a new and modern hotel has been erected – the Jules-César – and doubtless spoilt the monopoly: unless, of course, this third caravanserai is owned by the other two. In point of fact, the last time I was forced to feed in Arles was before the César was built and I had to content myself with a meal at the Nord. Indeed, I always try to avoid stopping in Arles (or Nîmes) for more than a stirrup-cup at the café. These towns live entirely on the tourist, thousands of which visit them annually, and when once one has seen the Arènes, St.-Trophime, the Maison Carrée and so forth, one may well seek material comforts in places less specifically engaged in the economic evaluation of spiritual needs. By the way, talking of these latter, the traveller who has not already been there, should on no account leave the district without visiting Aigues-Mortes – probably the most perfect mediæval town in all the world, quite unspoilt as Carcassonne is, by restoration. It is only an hour's run from Nîmes: I do not know what bodily content is to be found there; but I imagine it to be as meagre as the ramparts are magnificent. One can be well advised, however, to continue on to le Grau-du-Roi, 6 kilometres further on. In this quaint little port there is an excellent restaurant – namely, the Continental. I imagine that in the summer, at week-ends, it might be somewhat overcrowded; but at other times, one has the place to oneself, and the cooking is admirable. I can honestly recommend the bouillabaisse there.

From Arles to Nîmes is 30 kilometres, and the motorist must be careful to turn off to the right, out of G.C.15 into G.C.41, about a kilometre outside the town: as also, to turn sharply to the right across the level crossing some 7 kilometres further on. These warnings are necessary, as even the travellers knowing this road may make mistakes – especially after dark.

If one wishes to go directly to Montpellier and avoid Nîmes, one can take G.C.12, just outside Arles to the left, passing through St.-Gilles to Lunel. From Arles to Montpellier by this road is 73 kilometres: by Nîmes 81. But if the Arles-St.-Gilles-Lunel road is as it was last year (and for years before that) the longer way is the quicker. One can run a car upon G.C.12, but one can walk it almost as quickly. Of Nîmes, I have little to say gastronomically, generally avoiding stopping here for reasons cited above. When obliged so to do, I have usually stayed at the Cheval Blanc. It used to have a very fine table and is patronised – or was – by commercial gentlemen. The table is nothing like so good as it was a few years ago – before they put the baths in. In making for Bordeaux from Nîmes, one has the choice of two routes: the northern one, by

St.-Affrique to Albi and Agen: the southern one, viâ Montpellier, Narbonne and Toulouse. In respect to roads, I recommend the latter. And for another and very particular reason – namely, to enable the traveller to stop a night at Montpellier. This makes a convenient afternoon's stage of some four hours (about 170 kilometres) from Marseille.

This ancient town and University – whose school of medicine dates from the twelfth century – is, even yet, unspoilt by the ubiquitous English and American. Fortunately, the present town is of the eighteenth century – or seventeenth at the earliest and contains no famous monuments to attract the tourists. It possesses – besides the University – a Picture Gallery – containing a portrait, said to be by Raphael – and one of the most pleasantly placed gardens – the Peyrou – in all France. It is not in any degree what the Sydicat d'Initiative would call a 'ville musée,' and it is principally known for the famous men who have studied there – Petrarch having been a student there in 1320, and myself in 1913. For this latter reason, I hold Montpellier in very deep affection. No doubt, I am prejudiced in the matter, but to my mind, there is no town in France more agreeable to idle away a few days in than this, set as it is, on a high wedge of rock thrust out of the alluvial plain and giving one a panorama of the Mediterranean to the south, the distant Pyrénées to the west, and the southernmost spurs of the Cévennes to the north. There is a most comfortable hotel there: a more than excellent restaurant: cafés where one can idle away an hour very agreeably in decent company; and last, but not least, some old bookshops, where the

Curious may spend as much time as they can spare and spend as much money as their purse can afford. The hotel to stay at is the Metropole; an old house, modernised as to baths and so forth, but still preserving an old-time courtesy and restraint. One dines at the Brasserie Moderne on the Boulevard of the Esplanade – and one dines there as well as anywhere in this part of France – and as cheaply; for Montpellier is a town of Frenchmen – rentiers, professors and the like, apart from the students – who are not millionaires and, in any case, do not (as the French have it) 'feed their dogs on sausages.' Indeed, I know no restaurant serving its meals à la carte, giving such value for money as does the Brasserie at Montpellier. It is rather useless to give any details of dishes, though I might point out that the fish there is to be relied upon – especially the crayfish, the fishing village of Palavas being only eleven kilometres away. They also do an omelette lyonnaise there to perfection – a dish not so easy to do well as one might suppose. I especially advise the Thirsty Traveller to drink there the vin du pays rouge – en carafe. It is a very rare thing in France nowadays to find a sound local wine, served en carafe; the Brasserie Moderne is one of the few places I know of where such may be found. Before dining, one should take one's apéro' at one or other of the two big cafés in the Place de la Comédie, the Alsacienne, which is patronised by the students, providing a number of billiard tables (au fond) and the Riche, with a more select clientèle, and a band.

One may add that if the traveller, at any time, wishes to go sick, he can do so safely at Montpellier; possessing, as it does, the best faculty of medicine outside Paris and some of the ablest pharmacists in France.

I know of only one thing to be said against Montpellier. It enjoys a miserable climate, being bitterly cold in winter and scorchingly hot in summer. But then this is really a benefit, for it is an ill wind that blows nobody any good, and the ill winds of Montpellier are more than strong enough to blow all tourists (and such destructive insects) away. If the traveller comes to Montpellier in the summer-time, he may well spend a day at Palavas on the sea (vide supra). The bathing is perfect and fresh fish meals are obtainable there; although I do not recommend the Portugaise (Mediterranean oysters) there – or indeed, anywhere else. Taking the main road N.87 and N.9, one passes through Mèze and Pézenas to Béziers, but the traveller not in a hurry may well be advised to take the coast road – N.108 – to Sète (Cette), passing Frontignan, where the Muscat comes from. And if the Thirsty Traveller wishes to taste the best dessert wine made in France – the famous Muscat de Frontignan – he cannot do better than taste it here. Montpellier (naturally) offers of the best of this, but the finest I myself ever remember drinking was at a small and humble café in Agde, 23 kilometres beyond Sète, on G.C.38. The run from Sète to Agde, along the sand-ridge separating the Étang Thau from the sea is worth while doing in any case. Twenty-two kilometres from Agde brings one to Béziers.

I do not know if the tragic happenings in places – even in the remote past – can reflect upon the mind of the sensitive traveller to-day, so as to cause within him a distaste for any particular town. But for both Albi and Béziers, which were soaked in blood in the Albigensian war – some 30,000 persons being massacred in Béziers in 1209 – I have a particular dislike. And, indeed, there is little to attract the Gentle Traveller in modern Béziers, an ugly and somewhat shoddy-looking town, the centre of the vast and lucrative trade of making imitation clarets. The departments of Aude, Hérault and Gard produce nearly a half of the total output of wine in all France; and many a bottle of so-called St.-Julien, drunk in a Soho restaurant – or in restaurants outside Soho for that matter – grew its grape in the rich plains watered by the Orbe and the Aude and was vatted in the cellars of Béziers. None the less, one can eat well enough at Béziers, and I can especially recommend the little eating-house of the Chapon Fin, in the small square opposite the barracks. It is a humble place, but the food is excellent. Do not be put off by the clientèle, which is sometimes apt to be rough and noisy. You can get mullet and crayfish there as good as anywhere and game in season – and out, as far as that goes – your Méridional being a born 'braconnier': that is, one who defies the game laws.

From Béziers to Bordeaux, one has the choice of two routes: the northern one by St.-Pons, Albi and Montauban; the southern by Carcassonne and Toulouse. The latter is the better road: the former, more picturesque. To take the latter first, one can either travel direct to Carcassonne on G.C.11 and G.C.5, viâ Olonzac; or make the southern loop, through Narbonne, on N.9 and N.113. I recommend the latter; it is some 5 kilometres longer, but a better road.

LE BRACONNIER

At Narbonne, which is famous for honey, I have never eaten, so do not know what else may be got there besides honey. Of Carcassonne, I can speak more particularly from experience.

Speaking generally, I should advise the Epicurean Traveller to push on to Toulouse. Carcassonne lives upon sightseers, and after contemplating the restorations of Viollet-le-Duc it is not to be expected that one would take much interest in food.

There is, none the less, an excellent restaurant there (in the lower town), namely, that of Auter – with a speciality of foie gras. It should be noted that this house is closed from 1st July to 1st October.

If the traveller has been wise enough to spend the night at Montpellier and wishes to spend the next night at Toulouse, this gives him a very comfortable day's run of some 250 kilometres. He can then either lunch at Béziers or Carcassonne. At Toulouse, he can dine.

And he can dine well. But I do not recommend any of the hotels – gastronomically. The restaurant to dine at is chez Lucullus. It is said the patron, Bergeon-Jaillet, is as well known in Toulouse as is the Basilica of St.-Sernin. He well deserves to be – for there is no better cook between the Mediterranean and the Atlantic. To eat his cassoulet toulousien is to enjoy a real privilege; and his pâtés, and his hors-d'œuvres in general, are fully worthy of his reputation. As an example of what M. Bergeon-Jaillet can do, I cannot help quoting (from M. J.-A. P. Cousin) a special menu designed by this master. It reads as follows:

Les Hors-d'œuvres qui n'en craignent pas
Les Escargots d'Auteuil-Longchamp à la Bordelaise des Quinquonces
La belle Pièce de Bœuf en Daube
Omelette ou Œufs au beurre noir
Grillade pannée Maître-d'Hôtel aux Petits Pois sans façon
Entremets connus
Fromages
Fruits

There is only one thing to be said in adverse criticism of chez Lucullus – that it is sometimes apt to be overcrowded: especially on a Sunday. But with such elegant food at so moderate a price one can scarcely expect to have the house to oneself.

Of other eating-places in Toulouse, I have found the La Fayette, in the Place Wilson, quite pleasant in a straightforward and plain way.

From Toulouse to Bordeaux one can either take N.123 direct to Moissac and thence to Agen; or, alternatively, the southern loop on N.124 and N.130, through Auch and Condom, joining the main road to Bordeaux (N.127) at Port Ste.-Marie. If the latter road be taken, one can eat at Auch (at the Hôtel de France) in company with the officers of the garrison. But I do not recommend this to the Hungry Traveller – the garrison getting by far the best of it in the matter. It is well worth while, however, to stop at Condom. This gives one a pleasant little run of 120 kilometres from Toulouse before lunch. At Condom, one eats at the Lion d'Or, a modest house, but with an excellent table. Do not fail to taste the Armagnac here; Condom being the centre of the Armagnac distillation.

The traveller can take the northern route from

Toulouse, by N.20 and N.123 to Moissac – which was razed to the ground in the great flood disaster of the Tarn in 1930 – and thence to Agen – a total run of 109 kilometres. At Agen, he can lunch well at the Restaurant Festal – a good bourgeois house, but apt to be full of a week-end. Personally, I would make a little longer run of it and stop for lunch at Tonneins, 40 kilometres further on.

I know of few more pleasant houses in this part of France than the Hôtel du Centre at Tonneins. Madame Couret is an admirable hostess and sees to the wellbeing of her guests with the greatest solicitude. By the way, when I was last there, I was told that the name of the restaurant was being changed to Le Château and transferred across the square. The vin ordinaire – red or white Bordeaux – is remarkably good and cheap.

Another 100 kilometres and one arrives at Bordeaux: of which more later.

To revert back to Béziers, should one desire to take the northern road, cutting out Toulouse and passing by Albi, one takes N.112 from Béziers. Fifty kilometres brings one to St.-Pons and the Hungry Traveller can certainly eat there at the Hôtel Belot. Trout and game are commonly the order of the day there, and very good they are. The prices are also most moderate. From St.-Pons to Albi is a little over 90 kilometres. If the traveller has never been to Albi, he must, of course go there. Not to see the cathedral there, if one is at all near the place is to commit a solecism. But, like so many of the great 'monumental' towns of France, Albi does not shine gastronomically. The Hôtel Grand Saint-Antoine has a reputation and is supposed to be the best eating-house in the town. I have found the Vigan quite as good and one escapes, there, the grotto decoration that makes the former place so grotesque. But I recommend the Epicurean Traveller to spend all his time at Albi in its own and unique fortified basilica and seek material delights further away in some neighbouring town, less given over to Anglo-American sightseers.

FOURTH JOURNEY – ACROSS

CHAPTER FOURTEEN

FROM GUYENNE TO NORMANDY

THE northbound traveller who finds himself on the southern littoral as far east as Marseille, may be disposed to adopt an itinerary other than the well-worn one up the Rhône valley to Paris and beyond. He may be inclined – if he is fond of scenery and not in too great a hurry – to take a more circuitous route through Guyenne, the Limousin and Poitou into Normandy. If he chooses the late spring to do this journey, he may be well advised upon his attempt.

To the scenic fan, the route across the Cévennes, viâ Alais, le Puy and the Puy de Dôme, will have, no doubt, a particular appeal; but those savage and rocky uplands do not, as a whole, tend to provide the Hungry Traveller with succulent dishes and a bountiful board. Good inns are, of course, to be found; and trout, écrevisses and game (in season) are to be eaten in these regions; but taken, all in all, one would not specify departments such as the Cantal, the Aveyron or the Lozère as happy hunting-grounds for the epicure.

To the more gastronomically inclined, therefore, a westerly course might be indicated, viâ Montpellier to Cahors.

This former town has already been noticed in a preceding chapter, so I shall assume that the traveller has reached the old-fashioned town of Lodève some 50 kilometres along N.109, from Montpellier. This road is in an excellent state and affords some fine vistas for the observant. One passes through the somewhat dirty village of Gignac, where (I should imagine) one would find but poor entertainment. At Lodève, however, one may decide to dine and sleep with complete confidence. I can sincerely recommend there, the Hôtel du Nord, just off the place de la République. Coming from Montpellier, one crosses the river before reaching the centre of the town, which lies, for the most part, upon the further bank.

The Nord is an old-fashioned house which has recently been modernised as to running water, baths and so forth. It is clean and comfortable and has, moreover, an excellent kitchen. The night I stayed there, I had the set dinner, which consisted of a vegetable soup, a really beautiful salmon trout meunière, some of the best asparagus I have tasted recently, chicken and salad, cheese (a sound Roquefort) and fruit – all for the very reasonable sum of eighteen francs. The house also possesses a creditable cellar and I drank a bottle of Corton ('23) of considerable distinction. I also tried a local Marc – out of a mistaken sense of curiosity. It is the only thing in the house that I find myself unable to recommend from personal experience. One can, nevertheless, do as I did and descend to the common café and console oneself with a glass of any of the liqueurs de marque such as are to be found in all good cafés in France. One cannot hope to find old Cognac or old Armagnac or drinkable Marc everywhere. I was happy in finding in the old waiter who served me in this humble café, an old-world courtesy reminiscent of that 'vieille politesse française,' now, alas, but rarely encountered.

From Lodève to Cahors, by the direct route, is 238 kilometres, by way of Millau, la Primaube and Villefranche-de-Rouergue — which is famous for its cèpes — and passing over N.9 (as far as Millau) and thence forward on N.111. As some 60 kilometres of this latter road was marked in my Michelin 'State of Roads' map (winter '30-'31) with crosses, which indicates extreme badness, and having experienced the type of road marked 'mauvais,' I had no wish to encounter some forty miles of the 'très mauvais' order.

Accordingly, I took C.35 from Lodève to St.-Pons — passing through Bédarieux and leaving the 'spa' of Lamalou on the right. The first few miles out of Lodève is, by the way, a steep climb — more than 1200 feet being ascended in 4 kilometres. The view is proportionately magnificent. At St.-Pons (vide Chapter Thirteen) one falls into the 112th National route, at a distance of 74 kilometres from Lodève — and a good road all the way.

From St.-Pons to Castres is another 50 kilometres, the road being of the best. I lunched at Castres, at the

Grand Hôtel, in company with some officers of (I imagine) the higher command. The meal was fair enough – though scarcely, perhaps, quite equal to the uniforms. It included, none the less, an excellent brandade. On the whole, I was not much impressed with Castres, although I believe I fell upon the best hotel. A number of separate inquiries made, en route, all particularised the Grand, but without enthusiasm. Castres, I fancy, is somewhat after the manner of Auch – rather given over to the garrison.

From Castres to Cahors one passes viâ Gaillac. The direct road to Gaillac is G.C.83, but I was warned against this road and advised to make the détour viâ N.118 to Albi and thence on N.88 to Gaillac as being really shorter in the long run. From Gaillac one takes G.C.83, 32, and 22 to Caussade – all continuous and in fair condition. At Caussade one drops into N.20.

I believe one can feed very well in this clean and comfortable little town; but as I was anxious to reach Cahors that night, I only stopped there for a picon-citron. I hope to sample the skill of M. Larroque there another time. From Caussade to Cahors is 38 kilometres; the complete distance from Castres (viâ Albi) being 151. I know of few pleasanter towns in the south-west of France than Cahors and the entertainment at the Ambassadeurs is of the same agreeable order. The welcome here is most cordial and the service exact. It is a fine old house, with rooms discreetly modernised and an excellent kitchen. I especially remember some turbotin with creamed écrevisse and a fillet of beef, served and sliced, at table, in the English manner, which was agreeably tender. The house also has a well-stocked cellar, especially in respect to Bordeaux, though slightly on the young side. I was told that this cellar had only just been restocked. If the management are wise enough to limit their selling – which I doubt, for your tourist will drink anything with a name on the bottle – there should be some fine wine to be drunk in this house in some four or five years' time.

From Cahors, I decided to make for Poitiers. This makes a day's run of 313 kilometres, which can be very conveniently broken for lunch at Uzerche; thus making 138 for the morning's run and 175 for the afternoon.

The road is a good one (N.20) all the way to Uzerche and is particularly picturesque – especially between Cahors and Brive. It is a lush and fertile tract of country and Brive has a gastronomic reputation. I pushed on to Uzerche for lunch, however, as the latter place divided the day's run more equally. Also, I was anxious to investigate a house which, though of the humblest as regards size and accommodation, was honoured by Michelin with the rare distinction of three gastronomic stars.

This house is the Hostellerie Chavant. I certainly ate an agreeable meal there, including some excellent trout and asparagus, for the reasonable sum of eighteen francs. Perhaps I had expected too much, but I was certainly a little disappointed. I think the maison Chavant fully deserves to be starred – singly, but such a constellation as it has received tends but to excite unduly the appetite of the sanguine traveller.

From Uzerche to Limoges (a gloomy town) the road is first class. At Limoges one joins N.147 – perfect as far as Bellac. From Bellac to Lussac-les-Châteaux, however, the motorist will experience forty-odd kilometres of a French National route — utterly gone to pieces; and I know few worse things than this. Also, he will find this stretch of road — all the way from Bellac to Poitiers — which is 78 kilometres — almost as dry as England on a Sunday afternoon. I left Bellac without having satisfied my thirst (it was a warm day) and I failed to find a single café, en route, all the way to Poitiers, where I could even hope to find so much as a picon-citron or a vermouth-cassis or even a Pernod fils. I have fallen upon few roads in France so uncongenial as this to the Thirsty Traveller. Pocket flasks and independent springing is indicated in this part of Vienne.

But one reaches Poitiers at last — although shaken and thirsty. And here the stranger motorist will be faced with pretty little gyratory problems in getting in and about the town. When he has successfully solved them and found his hotel (I can recommend the Palais as a most comfortable house) he will no doubt be, by then, hungry as well as thirsty. He need have no qualms. He has come to the right place at last.

Let him make his way (on foot — it is quicker) to the Place d'Armes. He can conveniently take his apéro' there at one of the cafés in the square. Afterwards, let him adjourn to the Chapon Fin on the south corner of the Place. I have already spoken of the five first cooks in the provinces — the larger capitals being excluded: that is to say, the five first in my own experience, up to date. One always hopes to find yet another, worthy to be added.

M. Jean Bureau — ex-chef to the King of Norway

and the present proprietor of the Chapon Fin at Poitiers, is the fifth to be mentioned of these five aces. Again, it would be invidious to distinguish in merit between these five; but certainly M. Bureau is an equal of M. Caramello himself. One cannot say more.

The dinner I chose there – the menu is à la carte – was as follows:

> Hors-d'œuvres
> Bouilluture d'Anguille
> Goose, with a wonderful sweet sauce
>   of wine and minced vegetables
> Asparagus
> Cheese

The menu sounds less imposing than it actually was. The hors-d'œuvres alone might have made a respectable meal for a small eater; I remember particularly some very young and sweet onions, fresh mushrooms, écrevisse of an astonishing size and a rillette d'oie of a remarkable delicacy. The Bouilluture d'Anguille is a Poitevin dish and a speciality of the house. This is a dish of eels cut in chunks, and cooked in dry white Poitou wine, with cream and minced mushrooms. It is an old receipt and famous in the region as an essential in any wedding breakfast. The goose, needless to say, was delicious; as was the asparagus. With this meal, I drank, first some Mersault of '11, followed by Corton, Clos du Roi of '07. A wonderful evening – gastronomically – to be concluded with old Armagnac of a surpassing beauty.

M. Bureau was kind enough to give me the following receipts of a few of his specialities.

Le Saucisson Chaud du Poitou

Sausages of pork, cooked in dry white Poitou wine, together with minced vegetables, whole peppercorns and wild thyme.

Les Œufs Mollets Maison

Soft-boiled eggs, served in a small boat of flaky or puff pastry with a sauce of minced mushrooms and cream together with a purée of foie gras and sliced truffles.

Quenelles de Truites

The flesh of a filleted trout pounded and passed through a silk sieve, set in cream, and garnished with écrevisses.

Écrevisse

The river of Poitou provides numbers of écrevisses. The following receipt is a speciality of this house.

The écrevisses are to be brought quickly to the boil. A glass of good cognac is then to be thrown in and the cooking continued for ten minutes and to be completed with the juice of truffles and cream.

A Stuffing

This is a local dish made of sorrel, fat bacon and the soft crumb of bread, wrapped first in cabbage leaves and afterwards in a napkin. To be cooked in pork stock.

La Volaille à ma façon

A chicken, quartered, cooked with butter, fresh

minced mushrooms, the juices of truffles, madeira and cream, wrapped in puff pastry and cooked in the oven.

Le Poulet Poitevin

This is only to be eaten when fresh cèpes are in season. It is a chicken cooked with the cèpes that are abundant in this district.

Flan de Poires Poitevines

A cake of pears and nuts, served with a sauce of apricots and Kirsch.

The foregoing represent only a few of the specialities of this epicurean temple. I can most sincerely and earnestly advise the gourmet to sample them – even if it necessitates some divagation from his itinerary to visit Poitiers. Besides, there are other things in this historic town besides a restaurant – the façade of Notre-Dame-la-Grande, for example.

From Poitiers to Saumur, viâ N.147, is only about 90 kilometres. I was rash enough to attempt it without consulting my Michelin state-of-roads map and so had to crawl, painfully, all the way from Mirebeau to Montsoreau – a matter of over 50 kilometres. If possible, the road here was as bad as N.147 in Vienne, already noted. Perhaps being in the vicinity of le Mans, where the races are run, makes certain roads, unhonoured by the meeting, turn pitted out of spite?

I did, however, reach Saumur in time for lunch, which I ate at the Hôtel Budan. I can speak of this house in the highest terms, having been forced to remain there for three days with a fever; and although, perforce, limited as to diet, I was able, before leaving, to enjoy something of its excellent table. I was also able to taste some of the Saumur and Layon wines — particularly the Brèze and Beaulieu, of '20 and '21, the which I found much more agreeable than I had been led to expect from such bottles as I had already tasted, outside the region. Saumur is also noted for its castle and its cavalry school; and the variety of its uniforms adds a splash of colour to the place, particularly pleasing to the eye. Its cafés, needless to say, are exceedingly good and cheap; the cavalry sees to that.

From Saumur I made a day's run of 278 kilometres to Evreux, viâ Tours, Vendôme, Châteaudun and Chartres, on (for a change) a perfect road the whole way. Actually, one does not pass through Tours, as one leaves the Loire on one's right. I stopped for lunch at the hamlet of Freteval, 3 kilometres east of the crossroads, at Fontaine, of G.C.13 and N.10.

I feel I cannot be guilty of hyperbole in praising the modest inn of M. Gaspard in this tiny village. The place is small and humble, but spotlessly clean, and the cooking really remarkable. If any country auberge deserves three stars, this does. I had, there, hors-d'œuvres, including a delicious pâté maison, a vegetable soup, an omelette with fresh mushrooms, veal cutlets with green peas, a cauliflower, cheese, biscuits (of a particularly entrancing kind) and fruit. The price was not excessive at eighteen francs and the local wine, at a few francs a bottle, was as good as many (with labels on) that I have paid five times the price for. Indeed it was that very rare thing to find in France to-day, a vin ordinaire, of a sound grape and a drinkable age. The welcome of M. and Mme Gaspard was also most cordial. There is a dancing-floor outside, which I believe is patronised of a Sunday. But, as with many small eating-houses of local repute, I expect the house would be uncomfortably overcrowded of a week-end.

From Saumur to the cross roads at Fontaine (which is practically Freteval) is 132 kilometres, and on to Evreux, viâ Chartres and Dreux, is another 146. One follows N.10 to Chartres and N.154 on to Dreux. At Dreux, one branches to the right on N.12 as far as Nonancourt. There is an excellent inn here – namely, the Normandy – with a reputable kitchen: or, at least, it was so, five years ago, when I last ate there. This time I dined and slept at Evreux, 29 kilometres further on, northward, on N.154 again. As to Evreux, I dare say I found the best hotel in the place, but whether or no I found the best kitchen at the price is altogether another matter. No hotel could be more comfortable – indeed, almost luxurious – than the Grand Cerf. (By the way, I wonder how many Big Stag Inns there are in Normandy?) For the comfort and service provided, I do not think the charges exorbitant; but 50 francs for a table d'hôte dinner, is, in France (and especially in the provinces) a large figure. My dinner at the Grand Cerf consisted of an excellent cream soup, a turbot steak with sauce hollandaise, a choice between ham and spinach and tournedos and peas, asparagus, an ice, cheese and fruit – the latter including strawberries. It was (let me admit at once) a good dinner – but – all the same – a little, shall we say, undistinguished? I think – and I think that Sig. Pacciarella might think also – that, after all is said and done – even if one does have china cats on the roof and china dogs in the yard – Evreux is still a town of France, of comparatively small pretensions to being mondaine and not Brighton or Blackpool. He might even remember that fifty francs (in France) is a deuce of a lot of money for a meal, à prix fixe – even the great Point himself charges less for unique entertainment. . . . Fifty francs – 8s. or more – Lord bless my soul, I can lunch at the Ritz in London for less – and I most certainly do not expect to eat in Normandy Ritz-Carlton food at Carlton-Ritz prices. However, perhaps, it all goes to pay for the china cats and dogs – you can't (unfortunately) have something for nothing in this world. But then, I am not sure that I really wanted those dogs and cats. I feel certain that the bright young people – if they ever penetrate to Evreux, where there is a gothic monument that would no doubt depress them – they will be thrilled (or even th-r-r-r-illed and intrigued) with the Grand Cerf. Indeed, a party of them were the night I slept there and I had to ring for the night porter at one o'clock in the morning to restrain their enthusiasms. Dear me. It is a dreadful thing to grow old, is it not? But I am not sure that to grow young is not worse – it is so much more indecent.

From Evreux to Rouen is 52 kilometres; and if one is in a hurry to reach the coast one may go direct to Boulogne and Calais, viâ Neufchatel and Abbeville, along N.28. Dieppe, of course, is only a little over an hour's run from Rouen. I myself was crossing from Boulogne, but I made a détour almost into Dieppe in a spirit of gastronomic adventure. I was glad I had done so: for the Auberge du Clos Martin, at Martin-Église, is worth quite a lot of trouble to find.

To reach this hamlet – which is 6½ kilometres inland from Dieppe – one follows N.27 from Rouen until one reaches the village of St.-Aubin, some 6 kilometres south of Dieppe. One turns here to the right, taking G.C.54 and crossing N.15 to Arques-la-Bataille. One must take care, here, to turn to the right around the church and then to the left when G.C.1 is reached. From St.-Aubin to Martin-Église is altogether a matter of not more than about 8 kilometres. At Martin-Église there are two inns. I think I wisely chose the less pretentious one.

It was, happily, a fine and warm day and one was able to lunch in the orchard under apple trees in full bloom. M. Ruette, the owner and cook of this charming little auberge, possesses the *Golden Book* of the 'Club-sans-Club' – a distinction not given to everyone, which is in itself a surety of a good table. I had for lunch there, hors-d'œuvres, including a delicious pâté, trout, chicken and salad, green peas, cheese and strawberries and cream, for the quite reasonable sum of 25 francs. M. Ruette also has a creditable cellar – I drank a sound Burgundy – and his old Calvados is delightful.

From Dieppe (or Martin-Église) to Boulogne is 144 kilometres, with an excellent road all the way. From Martin-Église one takes G.C.100 passing through the village of Grèges until one strikes N.25. One then turns to the right following this national, through Eu, all the way to Abbeville – a distance of some 60 odd kilometres. Two hours' run from Abbeville should bring one to Boulogne. This road has already been detailed in Chapter One.

THREE CAPITALS IN GASTRONOMY

CHAPTER FIFTEEN

LYON

'Nous formons, ici,' said my barber of the Place Bellecour, as he paused, razor in hand, 'tous les élèves de Vichy.' Whatever degree of truth there may have been in such a generalisation, it is none the less true that one eats as well in Lyon as anywhere – to my mind, better than anywhere. Perhaps, my (shall I say?) rotundity had unduly impressed the hairdresser and he wished, as delicately as possible, to be cautionary. However, it cannot be denied that where the table is both of the best and the cheapest, some excess is to be anticipated. Even the gourmet is human; though that Vichy is proportionately crowded with the Lyonnais, I am unable to confirm; not yet having been there. No doubt my time will come.

But let us desist from such gloomy forebodings. Let us eat, drink and be merry, even if to-morrow we have to drink salt waters to the glory of the medical profession. Let us remember that Brillat-Savarin lived to be over seventy and many a nut-eater and milk-swallower has died in his nonage. Let us leave Vichy and the like to the valetudinarian. To-day we are in Lyon.

Of all towns in France, I fancy, sometimes, I love this busy town set upon two rivers, the best. Paris, of course, is Paris – but it is, to-day, sadly in the hands of the Philistines. Marseille is more expansive and colourful and boasts a better climate – despite the mistral: but it is more crowded and noisy and suffers, at least to some extent, from Riviera tourism and the P. & O. Your tripper does not go to Lyon; the which, although the third largest town in France, lacks, as yet a Cook's office. Indeed, the only cooks to be found in Lyon, are, I am thankful to say, of the culinary order. And their name is legion.

The central square of Lyon is, of course, the Place Bellecour, set equidistant between the Saône and the Rhône. When visiting Lyon, I am in the habit, myself, of descending at the Royal Hotel, in this square. It is a most central position and although a 'luxe' hotel, its charges are reasonable. Those wishful of a shade more luxury and anxious to conserve the inexpressible satisfaction of being a guest in one of the hotels of the famous international group which includes Claridges in Paris and the Negresco at Nice, can go to the Palace; but the situation opposite the Broteau station is not so central. Travellers by train are in the habit of stopping at the station hotel at the Perrache. This is convenient for the railway, but some distance from the centre of the town.

Lyon, with one exception to be noted in a moment, is an easy town for the motorist. Not only to get in and out of, but to drive within. This, no doubt, is partly due to the comparative rareness of taxis. Your Lyonnais is of a thrifty disposition and the cab industry in Lyon is not a flourishing one. Unlike Marseille, where taxis jam the traffic all day; a town as difficult to drive in as any I know, save, perhaps, Milan.

The northbound traveller entering the town has little difficulty, except to be careful to turn left out of the route de Vienne into the Avenue Berthelot and so cross the Rhône at the Pont Gallieni. Thence, any of the streets to the right brings him to the Place Bellecour, care being taken to observe the one-way systems indicated. Leaving the town for the north is also simple. One crosses the Saône by any convenient bridge and follows the river up on the further bank until one nears the Place de la Pyramide. Here, one may easily go wrong – I have, more than once, myself, although I know it by heart now – for the indications of the two routes out to Roanne and to Mâcon are a little confusing.

However, assuming that the Hungry Traveller has safely reached his hotel, it is to be considered where and how he shall dine. Your Lyonnais will tell you that you cannot dine ill in Lyon. With all respect to his civic pride, I humbly beg to differ. At least, it is quite easy to feed uncomfortably in Lyon, if one falls (so to speak) among thorns; and I only propose to concern myself with some half-dozen houses. There are innumerable 'petits coins' in Lyon, where the kitchen is beyond all praise (such as Léon Dean and Legroz) but they are tiny and crowded places, inclined, perhaps, to be a little antipathetic to the foreigner. Much about these and other like places is to be found in M. J.-A. P. Cousin's admirable book (himself a Lyonnais) and the curious gourmet is recommended to consult therein. Of the larger houses, the most reputed is, I suppose, Morateur. This old and famous house began life as a pastry-cook's about 1830. Thus, for nearly a century, this eating-house has added to the gastronomic lustre of Lyon. Morateur himself died in 1895 and the house is now owned by one of the family, a one-time barrister, M. Poirier. The restaurant, of a modest exterior, is situated in the rue Président Carnot, only a few minutes' walk from the Place Bellecour. Its inside is as plain and modest as it is outside, but its kitchen is exactly inverse to its décor. Your Lyonnais likes nothing better than to put the fairest picture in the plainest frame. He is the pure epicure, who, looking to the one essential, has no wish to be distracted from his delight in it, and would prefer to devour a peacock in the pantry rather than a chop on the Acropolis.

Chez Morateur, the diner is not disturbed in the serious and solemn act of eating by mural embellishments or orchestral symphonies.

M. Henri Beraud, the witty author of *Le Martyre de l'Obèse*, warns you upon the bill of fare:

>Si vous voulez maigrir,
>Ne mangez pas chez Morateur,

though this warning is not to be confined to any one eating-house in Lyon.

Among the specialities of the house are to be noted the following:

> Poulardes truffés
> Quenelles de brochet sauce Nantua
> Saucissons truffés
> Pâté de foie gras au Porto
> Filets de sole Morateur
> Langouste à la crème demi-deuil
> Langouste Bacchus
> Truite farcie braisée
> Volaille Béchamel de Théophile
> Poulet des Gourmets
> Poulet au Bourgogne
> Ris de Veau des Prélats

Certainly the cooking at Morateur's is a marvel. But it should be noted that the charges are (at least, for Lyon) somewhat on the high side. Also, it is wise to take M. Cousin's advice – 'eat only the specialities . . . do not go there for a steak and potatoes or a simple roast partridge.' Nor, may it be added, are the manners of the staff on an equality with the food. Maîtres d'hôtels and sommeliers should always remember that the lonely and modest diner is of more real value to a house than wedding banquets and the like. For one thing he is so very much more numerous. Many a fine old establishment has been ruined by a tip-hunting maître d'hôtel or a slovenly wine waiter. Which reminds me that the last time I dined chez Morateur, I was served with a bottle of Château Grillet, disgracefully corked.

Only a few yards away from Morateur, on the Quai de Retz, is to be found the house of Sorret. This, again, is one of the famous Lyonnais restaurants, and offers, among its special dishes:

> Langouste Belle-Aurore
> Truite braisée au Porto
> Truite Normande
> Volaille à la crème
> Asperges sauce midinette
> Bécasse Lucullus

There is also a set meal at 35 francs, which is to be recommended.

If one is in the mood for a brisk little walk of some twenty minutes before lunch or dinner (and what follows certainly demands a preliminary exercise) one can do no better than follow up the Rhône, crossing to the left bank by the Pont Morand and following the river until one reaches the rue Duquesne. Some half a kilometre along this street brings one to the restaurant of Mère Fillioux.

All the world knows (or should know) of Mère Fillioux. But for such as have never had the honour and privilege of eating there, a word or two to advise them of their loss should not be out of place. The original Mère Fillioux is, alas, dead. But the family carry on the house and conserve its great tradition.

This restaurant is egregious in more ways than one. In the first place, its service is wholly feminine – but of the mature and solid sort. No giddy, gallivanting, powder-puffing, lip-sticking Nippies wait within its sober and hallowed portals. Indeed, no Lyons girl is to be found (happily) in all Lyon. At Mère Fillioux's, a staid and respectable matron ladles out your soup and carves your capon, and the maîtresse d'hôtel (if one can coin the word?) is a woman of an ample presence, who has seen much of the world and one not lightly to be controverted. I only once saw her at a loss for a word and that was the last time I dined there. A gentleman who had not denied himself liquor, and had been making himself a nuisance for some time with a reiterated argument shouted at the top of his voice, was severely remonstrated with by this lady, who told him, amongst other things, that she knew well how to deal with *his* sort and that she had been there twenty-two years. His reply was: 'Well, madam, in another twenty-two you'll be somewhere else'; and he was left (for the time being) in command of the situation. But Mère Fillioux's is not only remarkable for its personnel; it is also apart in that it always serves the same dishes – or approximately the same dishes – day in, day out, year in, year out. M. Cousin, writing in 1927, gives the standard meal as follows:

> Jambon, saucisson, beurre
> Volaille demi-deuil
> Quenelles au gratin au buerre d'écrevisses
> Fonds d'artichauts au foie gras truffé
> Dessert

The last time I dined there – in February 1931 – there was (perhaps being winter) a slight change in the programme, which ran as follows:

> Chicken Broth
> Quenelles Nantua
> Boiled fowl with truffles and gherkins (demi-deuil)
> Fonds d'artichauts, etc.
> Glace Pralinée
> Cheese
> Fruit

The same, in fact, save a soup substituted for the ham and sausages.

Still, no sane man minds eating the same meal once in a while. Whenever in Lyon, one should not fail to have one meal chez Mère Fillioux. One would not go there, en pension, but to miss such cooking altogether would be the worst of solecisms. No boiled fowl is to be found anywhere as it is to be eaten here. M. Cousin states that 25,000 fowls are cooked at Fillioux's in a year and that they all come from Louhans, a town of some 3000 inhabitants in the Saône-et-Loire. I have never myself been there, but the place must be one vast chicken run.

I should add, by the way, that Mère Fillioux's cellar is beyond praise – the house is entitled 'Fillioux, Marchand de Vins.' I drank there last time some '15 Montrachet of a lovely quality, and the fine maison is to be thoroughly recommended. The fixed price of the meal is 40 francs. I suppose the Carillon is to be classed as one of the first restaurants in Lyon. Personally (and quite frankly) I don't care much for it. It was started in 1920, largely by the silk trade, as a rendezvous for foreign buyers and, perhaps, has, of necessity, a touch of the chichis tar brush. But it is honoured with four stars in Michelin, and M. Cousin has a good word for its cellar. Otherwise, he has little to say about it.

Another restaurant of a flamboyant order, that I cannot honestly recommend the epicure to patronise, is the Ambassadeurs, in the Place des Capucines. After midnight, it may be gay enough. But one must go there at the right time – for gaiety – and not for food.

Some years ago now, M. Moutet, than a député of Lyon (now, I believe, of the Drôme) did me a great service. He led me not only to what I consider the best restaurant in Lyon (the which, like good wine, I keep till the last) but also to the (apparently) humble and modest café-restaurant Debilly, at the corner of the rue Constantine and the rue Lanterne, in the older quarter of the town between the Place des Terreaux and the Saône. To any gourmet, wishful of eating in a small (but not necessarily crowded place) of the very best at a most moderate price, I firmly recommend this little café-restaurant. M. Curnonsky speaks especially of its hors-d'œuvres – to which I can myself testify – its snails, its pig's-trotters and mushrooms. I remember best myself its sole maison and its game – when, of course, in season. It has one small advantage (not common in Lyon where space is valuable) of providing chairs and tables without; so that, in warm weather, one can agreeably sip one's coffee and fine in the open air.

I have said that I keep the best wine until the end; and so, but a few paces from Debilly, I would lead the True Gourmet to the High Altar of Gastronomy, the house of Garcin, in the rue d'Algérie. M. Cousin places this old house at the head of his list of restaurants 'bien Lyonnais.' That he is right in his priority, I have not the slightest doubt. In fact, so much do I love this house that when in Lyon, I fear I favour it rather to the betterment of my gastronomic soul than to the lessening of my material girth. If Lyon raises pupils for Vichy, the house of Garcin may well be the most successful coach. For it is an eating-house, in which it is difficult to stop eating. . . . This restaurant, like Mère Fillioux's, conserves a feminine personnel – also of the mature and serious order. Its floor is strewn with sawdust, but its table is laden with the most alluring delicacies in all the world. Unlike Mère Fillioux's, there is not a set meal. The menu is à la carte. Where all is so excellent, it would seem almost insidious to nominate specialities – but one cannot speak of Garcin's without mentioning the 'sole au gratin' of the house. This (as are all such dishes in the house) is served in the dish it is cooked in: it is more a sole with cream and mushrooms and just a touch of cheese, than strictly a sole au gratin and it is worth while to travel all the way to Lyon to taste it. I have eaten the most perfect snails there, flavoured with basil and parsley, I have found anywhere. My last lunch at Garcin's was of snails, the above-noted sole, chou-fleur hollandaise, a chicory salad and real Marcellin cheese. This last, when the real thing – there are many imitations – is delicious; and, although of goat, by no means flavoured. The house of Garcin is famous for its meat: their entre-côtes, gras double, blanquette, bœuf braisé, etc., are unsurpassed. Their vins ordinaires – white and red – are also excellent. Needless to say the prices are amazingly low, and (an inevitable corollary) unless you arrive in good time for lunch you may fail to secure a table.

Yes: after mature reflection, I am not sure that I do not regard Garcin as the most perfect epicurean temple in all France – Paris not excluded. Montagné may be the Grand Master within the walls of Paris and Caramello without. Larue and Foyot may be more elaborate and the St.-Michel maintain the honour of Périgord. Isnard can serve you a bouillabaisse, and M. Godel conserves in Bordeaux an unique elegance. But for 'straight' cooking (bourgeois, if you will) Garcin holds, to my mind, the undisputed palm.

If, by the way, the traveller happens to visit Lyon in the summer-time, and is wishful of visiting a purely French watering-place, where he will scarcely be likely to find any of his countrymen, he can be well advised to go out for the day to Charbonnières-les-Bains, 11 kilometres to the west of the city.

There is an excellent little Casino there, pleasantly set in a modest park, with a good restaurant, where the Hungry Traveller is very comfortably entertained at a moderate cost.

If one is not anxious to drive one's own car, there is a continual service of motor-coaches between Lyon and Charbonnières, which functions until a late hour.

CHAPTER SIXTEEN

MARSEILLE

The second largest town in France is Marseille. Paris has a population approaching 3,000,000. Next to this comes the Southern Capital, with something over 600,000. Lyon runs this close with some 570,000. Bordeaux can claim less than half of this amount and the remaining big cities, Lille, Nice, St.-Etienne and Strasbourg are in the neighbourhood of 200,000. But Marseille is not only the second largest town in France. It is its second capital, situated, as it is, 500 miles to the south of the former. And your Marseillais is as different from your Parisian as is a Londoner from a Scotsman. Marseille is peculiarly French, perhaps more peculiarly French than Paris, but it is very peculiarly Marseille; with manners and customs, a behaviour, a dialect and a table especially its own. It is a city, therefore, of very great interest to the Curious Traveller. It is, perhaps, true that numbers of Anglo-Saxon travellers, for the most part brought thither by Steam Packet Companies, are often as indiscreetly curious as curiously indiscreet. But these, fortunately, confine themselves (as a rule) to the cafés of the Cannebière and are agreeably lost in a cosmopolitan crowd. They are unable to spoil Marseille and remain, together with other Nordics, Italians, Jews, Arabs, Turks, Greeks, Levantines, Indians, Negroes and every kind of mongrel and half-caste, as pieces of coloured glass in a continually changing kaleidoscope. Without these, Marseille would hardly be Marseille, and with them the Marseillais is born and buried, lives and dies, eats and drinks, works and plays, as regardless of the motley surging around him, as anyone might be of the moths that flutter round the lamp. Indian princes and English proconsuls jostle him in the street: the Riviera backwash floods the more flashy of his cafés: the sweepings of the Mediterranean basin litter his wharves, but the heart of Marius, as he eats his bouillabaisse and sips his clandestine pastis and argues vehemently with César the political issue, is untouched by any one of these.

Yet to the stranger Marseille is an hospitable place, less xenophobe, perhaps, than any town in France; and if the traveller is careful to avoid caravanserais, peculiarly affected by the English (there are two of them, whose unworthiness and avidity I do not propose to advertise), he should find his stay in Marseille an agreeable one.

The best hotel in Marseille – the best, indeed, I know in all France, considering the reasonableness of its charges – is the Noailles. With such inestimable eating-houses to hand, one does not, of course, eat in one's hotel; but I sincerely advise any who delight in cocktails to place themselves in the hands of 'Harry' at the Noaille Bar. He is one of the few barmen who are conscientious enough to serve his customers with a reasonably decent champagne in the glass. A small matter, no doubt, but one to be recorded; for I know nothing more pleasant than a glass of good champagne in the forenoon – and few things more disagreeable than a bad one.

Dulcis est disipere in loco – as the Romans have it; or, as I am used to paraphrase it, it is great fun getting drunk in the provinces. But this is only in manner speaking. Heaven forbid than any gourmet should forget his stewardship to the edge of intoxication. Yet, 'a man may drink and not be drunk' – at least, according to Bobbie Burns; and so, for the moment, I shall leave the strait and narrow course of eating-houses, and conduct the Thirsty Traveller to yet another bar.

If one walks down the Cannebière from the Noaille and takes the last turning to the left before the Vieux Port, one falls upon the Cintra. The bars owned by this company – which are similar (but I think much better) than those of the Bodega, are to be found elsewhere in France. There are two in Paris: the one by the Édouard Sept is, by the way, a first-class bar with purely a French clientèle – a rare thing in Paris. There is one in Nice – as already noted – and one in Lyon. This one in Marseille is especially pleasant, being large and roomy, with an outlook on the Old Port. If you are in need of a tonic, I can recommend their champagne 'pick-me-up' – a galvanic compound composed of champagne, curaçao, lemon, bitters and old brandy, to be taken (as required) in strict moderation. The Cintra also provides an assortment of side dishes – such as caviar sandwiches, egg and anchovies, prawns and capers, cheese and tomato, etc., to be eaten with one's apéro' – all very delectable, but apt, of course, to spoil an appetite for lunch.

The Cintra is the acknowledged meeting-place for the better class of business men in the town — although the ubiquitous English find their way there — and the house has the salutary rule that no unaccompanied female shall enter its portals. Even those, chaperoned by males, are not permitted to sit actually at the bar. Englishwomen, accustomed to Riviera hoydenism, will be reminded of their manners and that the feminine adornment of high stools is (in the real France) relegated strictly to demi-mondaine establishments.

Should the Thirsty Traveller wish to vary his morning pub-crawl, two other pleasurable and intime resorts may be indicated. One of these is Dan's Bar, in the rue Haxo. Dan has long been dead, but his widow has married again and, like the lady in the epitaph, 'carries on the business still.' This little bar is the peculiar retreat of the English business men resident in Marseille and is something almost of the nature of a club. The price of the drinks here is kept in very moderate limits. The other bar is that of the Brasserie Strasbourg, with a more French clientèle, and an entertaining barman, who used to be at the Cintra. It might be as well to add a note as to cafés, for such as are of a more conservative habit. The first of these is undoubtedly the Café Riche, at the corner where the rue de Rome meets the Cannebière. In winter-time the outer part is shut in with glass and warmed by stoves. The apéritifs of the French kind here are excellent; and the insular Briton might well overcome his prejudices for once and taste some of these. After all, Martinis, Manhattans and Bronxes, which are but vermouths plus gin, whisky or orange

LE PASTIS

may tend to pall. The French quinine wines are commonly mocked at by the English drinker (perhaps because they do not intoxicate quickly enough) but I entirely fail to see why folk who will swallow un-numbered 'pink gins' (to my taste, a foul concoction) should so sneer at them.

De gustibus, to be sure, but they may be a not unwelcome change to the ubiquitous cocktail. For a long drink, in summer-time, there are vermouth-cassis – a mixture of French vermouth (Nouilly-Prat) and red currant juice: picon-citron – a mixture of picon quinine wine and lemon 'sirop' – and gentian-Suze – all taken with water or soda water. Then there are the various forms of imitation absinthe – such as Pernod, Pernod fils, Berger, Marie-Brisard, Oxy, Amourette, etc., ... drunk with water. Of the short (or sec) apéritifs may be noted the two vermouths, French and Italian, St.-Raphael (red and white) Dubonnet and Byrrh. My own predilection is for (with long drinks) Pernod fils or picon-citron: with short, for white St.-Raphael; but this, of course, is a matter of taste. If one is happy enough to be a friend of the cafetier, one can, not infrequently in Marseille, and more easily in the country round about, obtain the real absinthe, privately distilled and sold, of course, *sub rosa*. The local argot for this is pastis, which means normally a 'mixture,' but is here applied always to illicit absinthe. Of other cafés, the Bristol is more cosmopolitan and the boule-vardier will find for himself such quiet and modest places as best please his mood. Needless to say, places flaunting titles such as 'American Bar,' 'English House,' and so forth, are drinking dens of the lowest type, entirely devoted to the fleecing of Anglo-Saxon sailors. No Marseillais or man of sense ever enters them. The same may be said (though the clientèle robbed is of the richer sort) of the after-theatre 'dancings.'

But to return to the more serious matter of good eating. The best restaurant in Marseille is undoubtedly the Brasserie Verdun, although Isnard runs it a close second and (for its specialities) is unsurpassed.

This house (the Verdun) which is in the rue Paradis, is certainly one of the best eating-houses in the south of France. Anything it provides is of the very first order, both as to material and cooking. The bill of fare is long and varied. There are two or three 'plats du jour' which can always be recommended. I have lunched and dined at the Verdun now over a period of many years and have never eaten a bad meal in the place. I can especially recommend its caviar, its oysters (marennes) and its pâté de foie gras, which are of the very best. As to dishes, one may note the following:

> Fish soup
> Langouste rémoulade (a caper sauce)
> Langouste Armoricaine
> Rouget grillé (with a sauce made of the inside of the fish)
> Côtelette de Mouton maréchal
>   (the mutton here is really tender)
> Dorade (or similar fish) flambée au fenouil
> Râble de lièvre
> Game in season
> Cèpes bordelaise
> Crêpes Suzette (kirsch and Grand Marnier)

I feel I must make a special note on the râble de

lièvre. This delectable dish, which is roast hare, is done here to perfection. The animal is first half roasted whole. The back is then carved off in slices, these being placed in a chafing-dish and cooked with a sauce made of its own blood, together with Oporto and brandy. I have never tasted its equal elsewhere.

As to wine, the vin ordinaire (a white Bordeaux), at 10 francs a bottle, is admirable: as to 'fine,' drink the old Armagnac. One should be warned that the Verdun is the favourite restaurant of the business men of Marseille and at lunch-time is apt to be filled by soon after midday. One should arrive in time to get a table or reserve it beforehand. Of an evening there is always plenty of room.

After the Verdun comes Isnard. This old and famous house stands a little way off the Cannebière in a network of mean streets: 4, rue Thabaneau is its actual address and it is the restaurant of the Hôtel des Phocéens. It is a small house, of a modest aspect, both within and without, but its kitchen and its cellar are of the first class. It has the oldest repute of any house in Marseille. Some years ago it became known suddenly to the English and suffered a severe relapse. This clientèle appears now, however, to have discovered fresh fields to conquer (or spoil) and, to-day, Isnard seems to have recovered its one-time famous quietness and worth. It is the house par excellence for bouillabaisse. If you want to eat this beautiful dish, go and eat it there. It is only served for lunch. The other great speciality of the house is sole Normande. I can also speak highly of its tournedos Rossini. It has, probably, the best cellar in Marseille. A Mersault may be indicated as accompanying the bouillabaisse. The fine maison is fully worthy of the house.

If one has disposed of too many of the extras provided at the Cintra and is in no mood to face a too serious meal, one can do worse than go to the Brasserie de Strasbourg in the Place de la Bourse. This house has improved greatly in the last year or two. It is an admirable place to go to for a dish of oysters or a grill. It has some excellent Lorraine beer and is open until the early hours of the morning, being a rendezvous for theatre people (from both in front and behind) after the show is over. An entirely respectable place, be it understood, where the early matutinal consumption of ham, eggs and shell-fish is taken seriously. It also has a reputable cellar. Almost next door to the Brasserie Strasbourg (but in the rue Papillon and beside the Strasbourg Bar) is the Restaurant Albert.

Albert Pizzi serves (or used to serve) by far the best hors-d'œuvres in Marseille. Indeed, one used to go there for a meal of oysters, hors-d'œuvres and cheese only. It is (or was) a first-class house. I am careful here to conjugate my verbs in two moods, for I do not think I have eaten chez Albert since 1927 or '28. I much regret it, for the entertainment was most agreeable; but I was driven away (as many old Marseille clients were also driven away) by the return of M. Pizzi's nephew – I believe that is the relationship – from America – to act as maître d'hôtel. Many disagreeable things have come out of America, but we cannot all emulate the philosophy of Dr. Pangloss and console ourselves with the thought that it is the price we pay for cochineal. I have a great love and respect for America, where I have spent some of the happiest times of my life, but the manners and accent that M. Pizzi's nephew brought back with him I certainly did not find in that hospitable country. Anyhow, they have successfully emptied the Restaurant Albert, and the sooner this is realised the better for the house. I, for one, should like to return.

No one who has known and loved a city well for many years can look back upon the changes that have taken place therein without some feeling of regret. 'Tout change, tout passe' is as true of Marseille as elsewhere; but, as he who died in Mesolonghi had it —

'There's little strange in this, but something strange is
The unusual quickness of these common changes.'

And one who knew Basso's in the golden age cannot but shed, metaphorically at least, a tear over its pinchbeck present. But it still preserves (I believe) its famous balcony and such as can support the mounting of so many stairs and such gastronomic misadventure as they may there chance to meet with, will at least be repaid by dining (in summer-time, of course) in the most glorious situation in Marseille. To sit and eat and drink upon this high ledge, looking down upon a forest of masts, with the last vestiges of sunset reddening the sea and sky beyond, with the frail lattice of the suspension bridge across the mouth of the Old Port, is almost worth the common pain of remembering Basso's as a rival to Isnard. However, we must move with the times, I suppose; and even innkeepers have to make a living somehow. Much has altered, even in ten years; and I can remember a lighter and gayer and (I like to think) a better Marseille, when, in summer-time, the Cigale on the Prado (now vanished) had something of the air that the Bullier boasted of, before it became Americanised. Of the Reserve, before it became the preserve of Anglo-Indian colonels and their encumbrances and was still the peculiar provenance of the discreet Marseillais, who wished to dine (perhaps indiscreetly) a little way out of town. Of petits coins intimes ... but let us also exercise a discretion. The snows of yesterday (as I have already pointed out) are all well melted by now – especially in Marseille. Our Indian Empire has seen to that. But by all means, go out to the Reserve. It has a position beyond all praise. Five years ago its set meal was marked at 25 francs: to-day it is 45. The food certainly is not better and the service is, of course, proportionately worse. However, there is always the view.

If I have been a little unkind to our Eastern Empire – and no one who has lived in Marseille can help being a little overcome by the exuberance of its administrators – it is only fair to admit that it has produced at least one admirable thing in Marseille – namely, the Cingalese Restaurant of the Elephant. To anyone fond of curries and similar dishes, this 'tea-room' can be honestly recommended – as also, for its tea. The cooking is really Cingalese, by a native cook, and not the usual fraud. It used to be in the rue Saint-Ferréol, but has since moved down behind the Place de la Bourse.

Of other houses in Marseille, one may note Flobert's. I have not eaten there for many years, but I believe it provides to-day a good meal at a modest price. Of Pascal's (an old and reputed house) I have no personal experience. By the way, the station buffet (Gare St.-Charles) is not to be sneezed at: I have fed there more than once, on catching a train connection. It is – or was – both good and cheap.

I feel I cannot leave the subject of Marseille without mention of one of its summer resorts – namely, Carry-le-Rouet.

This little fishing village with its quays and harbour, is one of the most charming spots to be found anywhere on the coast between Menton and Perpignan. It lies 32 kilometres to the west of Marseille and is served by the coast line running through L'Estaque to the Port de Bouc. By road one can take G.C.44 (as for Salon), but branching off at les Pennes into G.C.14 and later, to the right again, into G.C.15. The shorter way is to follow round the western waterside into G.C.30, which leads direct to Carry.

This village, which is made up of but a few houses clustered around the port, is backed by an extensive pine wood – on the edge of which is an old château, converted into an hotel. It is, alas, six years now since I was last there, but I still remember the Hôtel du Château at Carry with a deep affection. One lunched and dined on the wide terrace (I speak of July) and, then, there was no quibbling question of a set bill of fare. The cook, accompanied by a fisherman with a full basket, came to consult you in the forenoon – you chose what you fancied – rouget, langouste, dorade, poulpe, and so forth. You selected likewise your vegetables and your chicken. It was the perfect commissariat – as you had, indeed, been in your own house. The pension at that time, was 22 francs a head – all in!

You slept in a four-poster bed that had held a former countess, and you could do as you liked, dress as you liked, bathe as you liked all day. The hotel advertised water and electric light: but these only functioned on Saturdays and Sundays – for the week-enders from Marseille: it (very reasonably) not being considered worth while to use electric current – which also ran the pump – except for a full house. From Monday to Friday one had to be content (as our fathers had to be) with candles and water-cans. A delectable spot! I see, on referring to my 1931 Michelin, that the Hôtel du Château at Carry now boasts 40 rooms, all with running water, and two bathrooms – not to mention other conveniences. In the past, things were simpler; but I doubt, to-day, if you can get there your pick of farm-yard and fishing-net for 20 odd francs per diem. But one must march with the times – even in Carry-le-Rouet. *Illa sunt lacrima rerum*; and I suppose one must pay a price even for keeping clean.

CHAPTER SEVENTEEN

BORDEAUX

I AM afraid I cannot pretend to be fond of Bordeaux. I have stayed in this city a number of times over the last twenty years – the first time I went there was, I think, in 1913 – and at each visit I have liked it less. One can eat well there, and, needless to say, drink well. But as a common epicure – as one, that is, who regards food and wine, manners and custom, environment and that spirit particular to any city, as an acceptable whole, I have little love for the city of Bordeaux. I have much the same feeling for this capital as I have for Dijon. To my mind, at least – and I think the Gentle Traveller will be inclined to agree with me here – both these towns are a little spoilt by the wine trade. There is nothing like leather, of course; but one can sometimes have a little too much, even of a good thing; and in Bordeaux – as in Dijon – I always have a feeling that one eats and drinks there not so much to enjoy the fruits of the earth, as to be able to tell your friends about it afterwards. In Marseille and Lyon, one eats and drinks because one is normally hungry and thirsty – because one loves good food and fine wine – without any feeling of sitting down to a meal, as it were, on a stage. In brief, to use again that admirable word of

BAD WAITING

which there is no adequate translation in English, there is nothing of 'chichis' about Lyon or Marseille. Bordeaux is as full of it as an egg is of meat.

The home of 'chichis' in Bordeaux is the Chapon Fin. It has one of the best cellars in France, as is not unnatural, with MM. Suiet et Cie, 'négociants en vin' as its proprietors. It has the most hideous interior of any restaurant I know and a 'réputation mondiale' – which is about all that M. Cousin, for example, finds to say of it. Perhaps, there is not really very much more to say. Its kitchen, in my opinion, has degenerated considerably in the last few years. Its prices are, of course, high, and its clientèle foreign.

The second most famous eating-house in Bordeaux is the Chapeau Rouge. As to its table, I am not sure that it is not the best. Its prices are on the high side, but the food is well worth it. I know of no house outside Paris that preserves the elusive quality of 'finesse' so admirably as does the Chapeau Rouge. I have eaten a number of delicacies there, but the one that has stuck in my mind more than any other was tails of écrevisses à la crème. An entrancing dish. I have eaten the same, chez Point in Vienne, but these, here in Bordeaux, were certainly of a finer quality. The Hostellerie du Château-Trompette – in the street of that name, just off the Allées Tourny – has a great name, but I myself have no particular care for it. Its kitchen is good enough, no doubt – it should be at the price – but its manners to its guests are not such as to tend to enlarge its clientèle. One can eat as well elsewhere in Bordeaux – at the Restaurant de la Presse, for instance – where one is accorded a civil welcome.

Indeed, I prefer this restaurant (in the rue Porte-Dijeaux) to any other house in Bordeaux. Its Bordelais dishes are delightful and I have eaten the best eels there I remember anywhere. It has, also, an excellent cellar.

The traveller of a modest mind, who does not wish to parade at the more famous restaurants – especially if his purse insists on some economy – may well eat chez Jane-Madeleine, in the rue Buffon, just off the Place des Grands Hommes and but a few yards away from the Chapon Fin. Its service is à la carte – varied and well chosen – and the prices reasonable.

On the other side of the Place des Grands Hommes – in the rue Mantrec leading into the Allées Tourny – is the Basque Restaurant of Etche-Ona. It has somewhat pretentious décors within and even more pretentious prices; but it is the house in Bordeaux for Basque specialities. Those wishing a meal of the simpler sort can be recommended to the Restaurant de Madrid in the Allées Tourny. The Café-Restaurant of the Hôtel de Bordeaux (on the opposite side) also serves an excellent meal.

The lonely traveller, gregariously inclined, with something of the Boulevardier in him, will find Bordeaux a very dull hole compared to Marseille. The Bordelais has not, perhaps, the expansive spirit of the Provençal: his cafés are not despicable, but his 'bars' are miserable. They would scarcely do credit to an English provincial town – although the jeunesse dorée of the city certainly patronise them. I earnestly counsel the Gentle Traveller to avoid the chief of these – the Royal – opposite the Chapon Fin – where he will enjoy the worst cocktails at the highest prices and make the acquaintance of the second most disagreeable barman in France. The first, by the way, practises in Cannes. There is another house — the Lion Rouge — off the Cours de l'Intendance — which is much frequented by the gayer sparks of the town of an evening and is even more unpleasant. If one wants to drink a cocktail before dinner in reasonable comfort one should go to the Coq d'Or, in the rue Montesquieu. The American Bar is on the first floor, and the barman there is competent, as well as civil. Also, the place is not turned into a bear garden by Bordelais cubs. One can eat, by the way, well and at a moderate price, in the same house. Of cafés, that of the Coq d'Or and the Bordeaux are probably the best.

The motorist visiting Bordeaux in summer-time may wish to run out to Arcachon. It is only an hour's run, on a straight road — excellent when dry, but very dangerous when wet. Why this should be particularly so, I cannot tell. It is not a question of camber, but of the precise form of asphalt with which the road is surfaced.

There is a Casino — two Casinos in fact — and a bathing-beach at Arcachon; but a day there is all that the visitor will require. In summer-time, it is a sort of Bordelais Southend: in the winter-time, it is shuttered up and dead.

As to food, I have only eaten there at the Casino de la Plage. The meal was good enough, but no better than one would hope for in a Casino. I only know of two Casinos with outstanding tables — that of La Baule and that of Pau. The latter is worthy of the highest commendation.

In conclusion, one goes to Bordeaux to visit the vineyards and to drink claret. Obviously, one can drink claret to better advantage and in greater variety there than anywhere else. As a city, however, in which to spend agreeably any length of time, it is (at least in my opinion) a poor place.

SECOND PART
WINE LIST

CHAPTER EIGHTEEN

CLARET

It were impudent in any man to adventure upon so recondite a subject as that of the Wines of France after the exhaustive and authoritative work of Mr. Morton Shand. He who would acquaint himself with all the intricacies of this fascinating study can do no better than turn to these documented pages; as also to the delightful commentaries of Mr. Walter Berry, M. Paul de Cassagnac, M. André Simon, Professor Saintsbury and others – although the last (and first) named are apt to fill too many of us (I fear) with an envy of the unattainable. For the more detailed analysis of vintages, output and so forth, one can turn to the standard French works on the subject – such as the *Annuaire* of MM. Cocks et Feret of Bordeaux (a modest little volume of some 1200 pages), Camille Rodier on the Côte d'Or and so forth. There is then a whole library of books upon the cultivation of the vine – its botany, its physiology, its pathology – upon soils, roots, grafts, climate, pests – as, also, upon the elaborate chemistry of vinification. No man of sense would choose

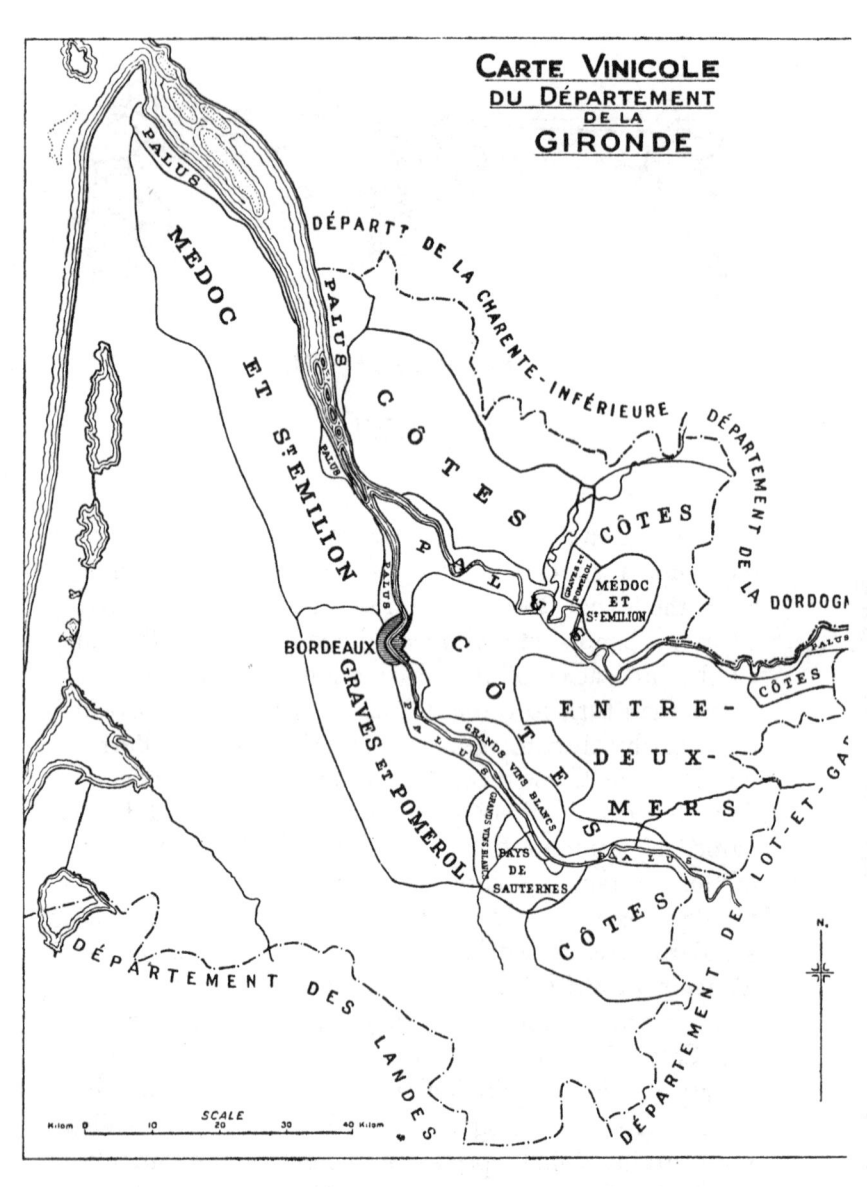

MAP OF THE DEPARTMENT OF THE GIRONDE, SHOWING THE
DISTRIBUTION OF THE CLARETS

to be didactic upon so vast a subject as wine without having mastered something of these origins; for to do so would be but to invite rebuke, and to place oneself on a level with the English Industrialist, who is but too often ignorant of the chemistry of the soap he sells or the dynamics of the machine that he constructs. Since I can claim no such knowledge and accomplishment, I do not propose to lay myself open to such rebuke in these pages. But to deny to a tract on what may be called Gastrography, some notes about wine, would seem to be at least ungracious to the general reader. For the convenience, therefore, of the epicure – unwilling to burden himself with too large a library – I append herewith, not a dissertation on wine, but simply a geography or classification of wines; so that, when the Thirsty Traveller sees a name upon a bottle he may, at least, have some notion of where the wine inside is grown – at least, as far as the label (or cork) is concerned. I have specially refrained from quoting the merits of particular years or the diverse qualities of growths: MM. Shand, Cocks and Feret and others having detailed this in full. It were foolish for the dilettante to dogmatise in such matters. So I shall very strictly confine myself, hereinafter, to the more exact and less debatable subjects of nomenclature and geography.

It is convenient to consider the wines of France as falling into three categories – namely clarets (Bordeaux), burgundies and other wines grown outside these specifically limited areas – such as the champagnes, the wines of Anjou and Touraine, of the Rhône valley, Savoy and the like. Let us take the clarets first.

These wines, grown in the department of the Gironde,

are generally entitled Bordeaux. This appellation, enforced by the law of 1911, includes all wine grown in the department, with the exception of the cantons Arcachon, Audenge, Belin, la Teste and Captieux and the communes of Carcan, Hourtin, Brach, Saumos, Lacanau, le Temple, le Porge, Lerm-et-Musset, Bourideys, Lucmau et Cazalis, Hostens, Saint-Léger and Saint-Symphorien: this exclusion consisting, roughly, of the sea-board of the Gulf of Gascony and the south-western corner of the department.

Bordeaux is generally divided up into nine districts – namely Médoc, St.-Émilion, Graves, pays de Sauternes, Grand Vins Blanc, Pomerol, Côtes, Éntre-deux-Mers and Palus. These limitations are shown in the Map on p. 208.

We may consider the Médoc first.

MÉDOC

The historic classification of 1855 divided the Médoc into five classes (crus) – including in the first, a wine, not a Médoc but a Graves – namely Haut-Brion. More recent classification has extended the list by categories of crus bourgeois supérieurs, crus bourgeois, crus artisans and crus paysans.

In the following list of growths only those classed in the 1855 classification, together with three, so to speak, on the edge thereof, and the principal 'bourgeois supérieurs' are noted.

The classification here following is that of the latest edition of Cocks and Feret (1929). The roman numerals refer to the crus in the 1855 list.

The châteaux are grouped in their communes,

CLARET

working downstream, from Parempuyre in the south to St.-Estèphe, nearly 40 kilometres further north. The output is given in tonneaux. A tonneau is the standard barrel of 225 litres capacity – about 300 ordinary wine bottles. The few white Médocs are unimportant and are not herewith noted. B.S. = Bourgeois supérieur : C.E. = Cru exceptionnel.

MÉDOC

Commune.	Château.	Class.	Output.
Parempuyre	Parempuyre	B.S.	35
	Ségur	B.S.	60
	Ségur-Fillon	B.S.	
Le Pian	Malleret	B.S.	30
	Barthez-Pian-Médoc	B.S.	
	Sénéjac	B.S.	60
	Bellegrave-du-Poujeau	B.S.	30
	Duthil-Haut-Cressant	B.S.	30
	Moulin-de-Soubeyran	B.S.	50
	Lamourous	B.S.	20
Ludon	La Lagune	III.	60
	Pomiès-Agassac	B.S.	100
	Paloumey	B.S.	60
Macau	Cantemerle	V.	100
	Trois-Moulins	B.S.	50
	Constant-Trois-Moulins	B.S.	30
	Maucamps	B.S.	50
	Cambon-La Pelouse	B.S.	40
	Rose-La Biche	B.S.	50
	Gironville	B.S.	20
	Priban	B.S.	70
	Bellevue	B.S	30
Arsac	Tertre	V.	100
	Arsac	B.S.	100
	Monbrison	B.S.	40
	Baury	B.S.	40

MÉDOC – *continued*

Commune	Château	Class.	Output
Labarde	Giscours	III.	60
	Dauzac	V.	60
	Rosemont	B.S.	40
	Labarde	B.S.	25
	Siran	B.S.	100
Cantenac	Brane-Cantenac	II.	150
	Kirwan	III.	100
	Issan	III.	50
	Cantenac-Brown	III.	90
	Palmer	III.	100
	Cantenac-Prieuré	IV.	30
	Pouget	IV.	30
	Angludet	B.S.	150
	Martinens	B.S.	75
	Montbrun	B.S.	25
	Pontac-Lynch	B.S.	30
Margaux	Margaux	I.	150
	Rausan-Ségla	II.	60
	Rausan-Gassies	II.	50
	Dufort-Vivens	II.	80
	Lascombes	II.	35
	Malescot-Saint-Exupéry	III.	50
	Ferrière	III.	20
	Desmirail	III.	80
	Marquis-d'Alesme-Becker	III.	25
	Boyd-Cantenac	III.	25
	Marquis-de-Terme	IV.	75
	Labégorce	B.S.	40
	Abbé-Gorsse-de-Gorsse	B.S.	50
	Abel-Laurant	B.S.	20
	La Gurgue	B.S.	30
	Lamouroux	B.S.	35
Avensan	Villegeorge	C.E.	20
	Citran-Clauzel	B.S.	160

CLARET

MÉDOC – *continued*

Commune.	Château.	Class.	Output.
Soussans	Bel-Air-Marquis-d'Aligre	C.E.	40
	La Tour-de-Mons	B.S.	175
	Paveil	B.S.	25
	Haut-Breton-Larigaudière	B.S.	40
	Haut-Tayac-et Siamois	B.S.	50
Moulis	Chasse-Spleen	C.E.	90
	Gastebois	B.S.	60
	Brillette	B.S.	70
	Poujeaux-Marly	B.S.	100
	Mauvesin	B.S.	80
	Pomeys	B.S.	40
	Gressier-Grand-Poujeaux	B.S.	40
	Duplessis	B.S.	150
	Anthonic	B.S.	50
	Dutruch-Grand-Poujeaux	B.S.	50
	Testeron	B.S.	25
	Moulis	B.S.	20
	Guitignan	B.S.	25
	Lestage-Darquier	B.S.	30
	Moulin-à-Vent	B.S.	40
	La Closerie	B.S.	25
	Bel-Air-Lagrave	B.S.	25
	Haut-Bordieu	B.S.	25
	Granins	B.S.	30
Listrac	Fourcas-Dupré	B.S.	110
	Fourcas-Hostein	B.S.	100
	Fonréaud	B.S.	150
	Clarke	B.S.	200
	Lestage	B.S.	150
	Saransot-Dupré	B.S.	140
Lamarque	Lamarque	B.S.	30
	Cap-de-Haut	B.S.	75
	Cartillon	B.S.	40
	Malescasse	B.S.	30
	Carrasset	B.S.	30

MÉDOC – *continued*

Commune.	Château.	Class.	Output.
Cussac	Beaumont	B.S.	75
	Lanessan	B.S.	150
	Lamothe-de-Bergeron	B.S.	70
	Bernones	B.S.	70
Saint-Laurent	La Tour-Carnet	III.	50
	Belgrave	V.	70
	Camensac	V.	70
	Larose-Trintaudon	B.S.	50
	Larose-Perganson	B.S.	25
	Barateau	B.S.	50
	Du Galan	B.S.	60
	Caronne-Sainte-Gemme	B.S.	80
	La Tour-Sieujan	B.S.	20
	La Tour-Marcillanet	B.S.	40
St.-Julien	Léoville-Las-Cases	II.	160
	Léoville-Poyferré	II.	120
	Léoville-Barton	II.	150
	Gruaud-Larose-Sarget	II.	150
	Gruaud-Larose-Faure	II.	100
	Beaucaillou	II.	150
	Lagrange	III.	200
	Langoa	III.	100
	Saint-Pierre-Bontemps	IV.	40
	Saint-Pierre-Sevaistre	IV.	60
	Branaire-Ducru	IV.	100
	Talbot	IV.	150
	Beychevelle	IV.	160
	Moulin-Riche	B.S.	55
	Médoc	B.S.	80
Pauillac	Lafite	I.	150
	Latour	I.	100
	Mouton-Rothschild	II.	150
	Pichon-Longueville	II.	78
	Pichon-Longueville Comtesse de Lalande	II.	100

CLARET 215

MÉDOC – *continued*

Commune.	Château.	Class.	Output.
Pauillac	Duhart-Milon	IV.	140
	Pontet-Canet	V.	200
	Batailley	V.	50
	Grand-Puy-Ducasse	V.	40
	Grand-Puy-Lacoste-Saint-Guirons	V.	120
	Lynch-Bages	V.	130
	Lynch-Moussas	V.	20
	Mouton-d'Armailhacq	V.	250
	Calvé-Croizet-Bages	V.	50
	Haut-Bages-Libéral	V.	40
	Pédesclaux	V.	40
	Clerc-Milon-Mondon	V.	35
	Couronne	B.S.	30
	Constant-Bages-Monpelou	B.S.	50
	Colombier-Monpelou	B.S.	100
	Malecot	B.S.	75
	Balogues-Haut-Bages	B.S.	100
	Bellegrave	B.S.	55
	Bellevue-Saint-Lambert	B.S.	40
	Bellevue-Cordeillan-Bages	B.S.	25
	Padarnac	B.S.	20
	Fonbadet	B.S.	80
	Bichon-Bages	B.S.	60
	Daubos-Haut-Bages	B.S.	20
	Haut-Bages-Drouillet	B.S.	20
	Haut-Milon	B.S.	40
	La Tour-Milon	B.S.	60
	Carruades	B.S.	50
	Montloubède-Milon	B.S.	20
Saint-Sauveur	Liversan	B.S.	150
	Fonpiqueyre	B.S.	50
	Madrac	B.S.	45
	Tourteran	B.S.	60
Saint-Estèphe	Cos d'Estournel	II.	150

MÉDOC – *continued*

Commune	Château	Class	Output
Saint-Estèphe	Montrose	II.	100
	Calon-Ségur	III.	225
	Rochet	IV.	100
	Cos Labory	IV.	45
	Le Roc	B.S.	40
	Tronquoy-Lalande	B.S.	130
	Meyney	B.S.	175
	Le Crock	B.S.	125
	Marbuzet	B.S.	80
	Le Boscq	B.S.	180
	Beau-Site	B.S.	100
	Roche	B.S.	60
	Fatin	B.S.	90
	Fonpetite	B.S.	100
	Phélan-Ségur	B.S.	150
	Pez	B.S.	40
	Houissant	B.S.	40
	Canteloup	B.S.	110
	Capbern	B.S.	5
	Clos-Saint-Estèphe	B.S.	25
	Pomys	B.S.	40
	Picard	B.S.	60
	Beauséjour	B.S.	50
	La Haye	B.S.	30
	Clauzet	B.S.	30
	Morin	B.S.	70
	La Commanderie	B.S.	80
	Les Ormes-de-Pez	B.S.	80
	Ladouys	B.S.	40
	Coutelin-Merville	B.S.	60
	Mac-Carthy	B.S.	40
	Maccarthy-Moula-Marbuzet	B.S.	35
	Saint-Estèphe	B.S.	35
	Plantier-Rose	B.S.	50
	La Tour des Termes	B.S.	25

CLARET

MÉDOC – *continued*

Commune.	Château.	Class.	Output.
Saint-Estèphe	Laffitte-Carcasset-Saint-Estèphe	B.S.	60
	Moulin de Calon	B.S.	50
	Andron-Blanquet	B.S.	30

GRAVES

Upstream, and still on the left bank of the Gironde, one passes from the district of the Médoc into the Graves. These growths have no formal classification such as the Médocs have, but the principal ones are quoted below under their respective communes. As many of the most famous Graves are red – e.g. Haut Brion, Pape Clément, etc. – the colour of the growth is stated. It may, perhaps, be as well to point out that white wine is not necessarily made from white grapes. Many white wines (champagne, for example) are made from red grapes. The red colour in wine comes from the skin, which if removed before fermentation leaves a white wine to be produced. To avoid too extended a list, a number of the smaller, but quite excellent, growths have been perforce omitted.

GRAVES

Commune.	Château.	Output. Red.	White.
Pessac	Haut-Brion	100	
	(Generally classed with Médoc I – 1855 Classification)		
	Mission Haut-Brion	35	
	Pape Clément	80	
	Bellegrave	10	
	Camponac		

GRAVES – *continued*

Commune.	Château.	Red.	White.
Pessac	Carmes-Haut-Brion	12	
	Phénix	10	
	Fanning-Lafontain	15	
Talence	La Tour-Haut-Brion	15	
	Raba	15	
Mérignac	Bon-Air, La Tour-du-Pape	25	
Le Haillan	Bel-Air	40	
Villenave-d'Ornon	Baret	80	25
	La Haye-Pullès	65	45
	Carbonnieux	150	120
	Duc-d'Épernon		30
	Pontac-Monplaisir	80	
	Couhins	30	
	Lahontan	50	6
	Haut-Madère	10	
	Clos Cantebau		25
	Terrefort de Fortissan	40	10
Gradignan	Lafon	10	
	Lange	15	
	Laurenzane	100	
	Barthez	20	
Leognan	Haut-Bailly	60	
	Malartic-Lagravière	40	
	Dom. de Chevalier	30	
	Larrivet-Haut-Brion	30	
	Fieuzal	30	15
	Carbonnieux	150	120
	Haut-Gardère	50	10
	Rigaillhou	35	
	Olivier	120	12
	La Louvière	85	40
	Brown	40	60
	Dom. de Grandmaison	20	10
	Le Pape	15	

GRAVES – *continued*

Commune.	Château.	Output. Red.	White.
Martillac	Smith-Haut-Laffitte	50	10
	La Garde	100	
	Ferran	60	20
	Nouchet	30	10
	L'Hermitage	45	
	Saint-Augustin-La-Grave	208	
Begles	de Hilde	50	
Cadaujac	Brésil	90	
	Lamothe-Bouscaut	15	
	Maleret	50	
	Bouscaut		50
St.-Médard-d'Eyrans	Lafargue	10	15
Ayguemorte-les-Graves	Lusseau	40	20
	Méjan	25	10
Castres	Pommarède	20	8
Saucats	Grand-Laguloup	30	10
Portets	Millet	50	10
	Lognac	50	
	Portets	25	25
	Cabannieux	20	10
	Pessan	18	10
	La Tour-Bicheau	35	
Arbanats	Tourteau-Chollet-Laffitte	20	40
	Arbanats	5	30
Landiras	d'Arricaud		25

GRANDS VINS BLANCS (SAUTERNES, BOMMES, BARSAC, ETC.)

Moving still further south, along the river, one comes to the region of the Sauternes and Barsacs and their congeners. These were classified in 1855, as were the Médocs, but in two classes only. In the following list, the roman numerals refer to this. The better growths, not so listed, are noted as B.S. (Bourgeois Supérieur). The production of red wines in these districts is small.

GRANDS VINS BLANCS (SAUTERNES, BOMMES, BARSAC, ETC.)

Commune.	Château.	Class.	Output.
Sauternes	Yquem	I.	125
	Guiraud	I.	80
	Raymond-Lafon	B.S.	14
	d'Arche-Lagaurie	II.	15
	d'Arche	II.	10
	Lafon	B.S.	12
	Filhot	II.	70
	Lamothe	II.	14
Bommes	La Tour-Blanche	I.	40
	Lafaurie-Peyraguey	I.	35
	Rayne-Vigneau	I.	75
	Rabaud-Promis	I.	35
	Sigalas-Rabaud	I.	35
	Haut-Peyraguey	I.	15
Barsac	Coutet	I.	60
	Climens	I.	45
	Myrat	II.	40
	Doisy-Dubroca	II.	15
	Doisy-Védrines	II.	40
	Doisy-Daëne	II.	8
	Cantegril	B.S.	20
	Suau	II.	15
	Broustet	II.	30
	Caillou	II.	45
	Piada	B.S.	18
	Roumieux	B.S.	18

CLARET

GRANDS VINS BLANCS, ETC. — *continued*

Commune.	Château.	Class.	Output.
Barsac	Carles	B.S.	15
	Nairac	II.	30
	de Rolland	B.S.	16
	Bastard	B.S.	15
	Dudon	B.S.	25
	Liot	B.S.	30
	Hallet	B.S.	50
	Camperos	B.S.	37
	Mayne-Bert	B.S.	37
Preignac	Suduiraut	I.	75
	Malle	II.	25
	Bastor-Lamontagne	B.S.	70
	Rochers	B.S.	20
	d'Armajan-des-Ormes	B.S.	10
Fargues	Rieussec	I.	60
	Romer-Lafon	II.	20
	Peyron	B.S.	20
Saint-Pierre-du Mons	Respide	B.S.	30
Cérons	Calvimont	B.S.	30
	Cérons	B.S.	15
	Grand-Chemin	B.S.	20
	Le Mayne	B.S.	30

ST.-ÉMILION AND POMEROL

Crossing to the right bank of the Gironde from the Sauternes district and moving northward across the intervening districts of the Côtes and the Entre-Deux-Mers one crosses to that tributary of the Gironde — the Dordogne. Crossing this latter at Braune, one reaches the region of the St.-Émilions, with that of Pomerol to the north-west. Following herewith are the chief first growths of the St.-Émilion — together with those of the Graves-St.-Émilion and the Pomerol. For reasons of space, the so-called second-first growths and the second growths have not been cited. These wines are all red.

ST. ÉMILION — I. CRUS

Château.	Output.
Ausone	15
Bélair et Chapelle Madeleine	30
Magdelaine	20
Canon	75
Fourtet	50
Beauséjour	40
Saint-Georges-Côte-Pavie	20
Pavie	200
Fonplégade	35
Pavie-Macquin	70
Pavie-Decesse	25
Tertre-Daugay	30
Tertre-Daugay-de Vassal	25
Berliquet	35
Villemaurine	28
Cadet-Piola	15
Cadet-Bon	30
Haut-Cadet	25
Soutard	100
Troplong-Mondot	120
Coutet	40
Bellevue	30
La Gaffelière-Naudes	50
La Clotte de Grailly	20
Sansonnet	40
Petit-Faurie-de-Soutard	50
Trottevieille	30
La Couspaude	40
Fonroque	80

ST. ÉMILION — I. CRUS — *continued*

Château.	Output.
Balestard-la-Tonnelle	30
Bragard	30
Malineau	20
Canon-La Gaffelière	45
Saint-Émilion	25
l'Angélus	100
Baleau	50
Franc-Mayne	30
Grand-Mayne	75
Laniote	30
Guadet-Saint-Julien	35
Saint-Julien	25
Mourlin	30
La Clotte-Grand-Côte	20
Mazerat	30
Trimoulet	25
Haut-Pourret	10
Franc-Pourret	35

GRAVES-ST.-ÉMILION — I. CRUS

Cheval-Blanc	100
Figeac	150
La Dominique	40
Ripeau	40
La Tour-Figeac	70
La Tour-du-Pin-Figeac	35
La Tour-du-Pin-Figeac-Ströhl	40
Dom. de Figeac	20
Grand-Barrail-Lamarzelle-Figeac	135
La Marzelle	30
Croque-Michotte	40
Corbin-Michotte	50
Corbin	50
Jean Faure	30

SAINT-ÉMILION–SAINT-CHRISTOPHE-DES-BARDES — I. CRUS

Château.	*Output.*
Haut-Sarpe	25
Gaubert	30
Pelletan	20
Fombrauge	80

SAINT-ÉMILION — SAINT-LAURENT-DES-COMBES — I. CRUS

Larcis-Ducasse	80
Clos La Barde	20
Bellefond-Belcier	85
La Barde	35
Tertre-Bellevue	15
La Bouygue	20
Cru Bourbaine	25

POMEROL — I. CRUS

Pétrus	35
Vieux-Château-Certan	40
l'Évangile	45
La Conseillante	40
Petit-Village	45
Trotanoy	25
Clos des Grandes Vignes et Ch. Latour-Pomerol réunis.	40
Guillot	20
Clos l'Église	25
Dom. de la Grave-Trigant-de-Boisset	25
La Fleur-Pétrus	20
Beauregard	35
Nénin	100
Gazin	80
Le Gay	25
Clos de l'Église-Clinet	30
Dom. de l'Église	20

CLARET

POMEROL – I. CRUS – *continued*

Château.	Output.
Lacabanne	50
Bougneuf	40
La Pointe	60
Clinet	35
Feytit-Clinet	25
Rouget	35
La Croix	30
Grate-Cap	30
Gombaude-Guillot	35

This concludes the principal growths of Bordeaux. Of the vast number of growths, outside the already quoted limitations – such as those of the Côtes, the Entre-deux-Mers and the Palus, it is not within the scope of this book to detail.

CHAPTER NINETEEN

BURGUNDY

The wines of Burgundy present a much more complicated problem than do the wines of Bordeaux, but they may be roughly divided into three categories, namely:

(*a*) Those of the Côte d'Or (true Burgundies).
(*b*) Those of the Dept. of the Yonne, i.e., Chablis.
(*c*) Those of the districts south of the Côte d'Or along the Saône – viz., Chalonnais, Mâconnais and Beaujolais.

I shall not detail the last two categories, but confine myself to a list (abridged) of the growths of the Côte d'Or or Burgundy proper.

The Côte d'Or vineyards rest on the slope of the hills on the right-hand side of the road running down (roughly) from Dijon to Chagny. In the following list, the communes are arranged in this order. The classification observed is that of M. Camille Rodier: growths cited as 'Tête de Cuvée' by Mr. Morton Shand, being printed in capitals. Vineyard areas are given in acres;

and only the first and second growths are quoted – in some cases only the first. Many omissions have been necessary in respect of space.

It must be borne in mind that Burgundy growths are seldom held by one owner, but are split up among a number. For example, Aux Argillats, a second cuvée of the Nuits, divides its 6 acres among 33 proprietors; (1920) or an average of less than one-fifth of an acre per proprietor. Estate bottling is not the practice in Burgundy, as it is in the majority of cases in Bordeaux, where vineyards are much larger and singly owned. There are exceptions – M. Louis Latour being a notable one. The majority of Burgundy – even true and undoctored Burgundy – is, perforce, a mixture of a number of cuvées approximating to a particular quality and taste; and almost as much a blended wine as champagne; and to be sure of drinking a pure and undiluted wine of one of the small and famous growths is not always easy – save in cases where the property is in the hands of a single owner; or (if divided up) where the wine is obtained directly from one of the proprietors.

(A) CÔTE DE DIJON

Commune.	I Cuvée.	II Cuvée.	Area.
CHENÔVE		Chapitre	15
		Clos du Roi	64
FIXEY	Les Arvelets		8
FIXEY		La Mazière	5
		Champennebaut	2
		Les Mogottes	4
FIXIN	LA PERRIÈRE		12
	Le Chapitre		12
		En Combe-Roy	2

(B) CÔTE DE NUITS

Commune.	I Cuvée.	II Cuvée.	Area.
GEVREY-CHAMBERTIN	LE CHAMBERTIN (including CLOS DE BEZE)		67
		Les Latricières	17
		Aux Charmes	30
		Mazoyères	36
		Aux Combottes	13
		Saint-Jacques	6
		Les Varoilles	15
		La Chapelle	20
		Les Mazis-Hauts	11
		Ruchottes-du-Dessus	8
		La Grillotte	7
		Les Cazetiers	20
MOREY	CLOS DE TART		17
	Clos des Lambrays		22
	Clos de la Roche		11
	Clos Saint-Denis		5
	Chabiots		5
	Les Chaffots		10
	Les Millandes		11
	Clos des Ormes		13
	Les Chenevery		8
		Clos Sorbet	8
		Les Sorbet	8
		La Bussière	8
		Les Ruchots	7
		La Riotte	6
		Les Monts-Luisants	29
CHAMBOLLE-MUSIGNY	LES MUSIGNY		14
	LES BONNES-MARES		34
	Les Petits-Musigny		10
	La Combe d'Orveau		15

(B) CÔTE DE NUITS – *continued*

Commune.	I Cuvée.	II Cuvée.	Area.
CHAMBOLLE-MUSIGNY	Les Fuées		11
	Les Cras		18
	Les Baudes		9
	Les Amoureuses		13
	Les Hauts-Doix		4
	Les Charmes		15
	Les Sentiers		10
		Les Condemènes	12
		Les Noirets	7
		Les Beaux-Bruns	6
		Les Bussières	10
		Les Châtelots	6
		Les Combottes	5
		Aux Croix	6
		Les Drazey	9
		Les Échezeaux	6
		Les Feusselottes	12
		Les Fremières	11
GILLY-LES-VOUGEOTS	·CLOS DE VOUGEOT		125
		Les Petits-Vougeots	19
		Les Cras	11
FLAGEY-ÉCHEZEAUX	LES GRANDS ÉCHEZEAUX		23
	Les Échezeaux-du-Dessus		9
	En Orveau		25
	Les Poulaillères		17
	Les Loachausses		8
	Les Cruots		8
	Les Champs-Traversins		9
	Les Rouges-du-Bas		7
	Les Beaux-Monts-Bas		14
	Le Clos Saint-Denis		5
	Les Qurtiers-de-Nuits		6
	Les Treux		12

(B) CÔTE DE NUITS – *continued*

Commune.	I Cuvée.	II Cuvée.	Area.
FLAGEY-ÉCHEZEAUX		Les Beaumonts-Hauts	4
		Les Haut-Mazières	3
		Les Rouges-Dessus	9
VOSNE-ROMANÉE	LA ROMANÉE-CONTI		4½
	LA ROMANÉE		2
	LA ROMANÉE-ST.-VIVANT		23
	LES RICHEBOURG		12
	LA TACHE		3½
	Les Veroilles-ou-Richebourg		9
	Les Malconsorts		15
	Les Gaudichots		14
	La Grande-Rue		3
	Les Beaumonts		6
	Aux Brulées		9
	Les Suchots		33
	Aux Reignots		4
	Aux Petits-Monts		9
		Les Chaumes	18
		Clos de Réas	5
		Aux Réas	24
		Les Hautes-Maizières	14
		Les Hauts-Beaumonts	9
		La Combe-Brûlée	4
		Aux Cros Parantoux	2½
		Au-dessus-des-Malconsorts	2½
		Derrière-le-Four	4
NUITS-SAINT-GEORGES	LES SAINT-GEORGES		20
	LES CAILLES		10
	Les Vaucrains		15

(B) CÔTE DE NUITS – *continued*

Commune.	I Cuvée.	II Cuvée.	Area.
NUITS-SAINT-GEORGES	Les Pruliers		30
	Les Porrets		17
	Aux Murgers		10
	Aux Cras		7
	Aux Boudots		15
	Les Richemonnes		5
	Aux Chaignots		12
	Aux Rousselots		11
	La Perrière		10
	Les Poulettes		6
		Les Chaînes-Carteaux	7
		Les Vallerots	24
		Les Plateaux	20
		Aux Argillats	6
		Aux Torey	15
		Aux Vignerondes	8
		Aux Lavières	15
		Au Bas-de-Combe	14
PREMEAUX	Les Didiers		7
	Les Forêts		13
	Les Corvées		19
	Les Corvées-Paget		3
	Les Perdrix		8
	Clos Saint-Marc		7
	Clos-des-Argillières		12
	Clos Arlot		19
	Clos de la Maréchale		24
		Les-Plantes-au-Baron	7
		Les Petits-Plets	6
		Aux Tapones	9
		Les Charbonnières	12
		Les Grandes-Vignes	10

(B) CÔTE DE NUITS — *continued*

Commune.	I Cuvée.	II Cuvée.	Area.
PREMEAUX		Clos des Leurées	12
LADOIX-SERRIGNY	Rouget-et-Corton		23
	Les Vergennes		3
		Les Lolières	10
		La Coutière	6
		La Tope-au-Vert	5

(C) CÔTE DE BEAUNE

Commune.	I Cuvée.	II Cuvée.	Area.
ALOXE-CORTON	LE CORTON		28
	CLOS DU ROI		26
	Les Renardes		37
	Les Bressandes		42
	Les Pougets		24
	Les Languettes		18
	Les Perrières		27
	Les Grèves		5
	En Charlemagne		41
	Les Chaumes		17
PERNAND	Ile des Vergelesses		23
	Les Basses-Vergelesses		44
		En Charlemagne	49
		En Caradeux	50
		Creux-de-la-Net	12
		Les Fichots	27
SAVIGNY-LES-BEAUNE	Les Vergelesses		42
	Les Marconnets		22
	Les Jarrons		25
	Les Narbantons		33
	Aux Gravains		16
	Les Lavières		46
	Les Peuillets		57
	Aux Guettes		53
	Les Talmettes		8

BURGUNDY 233

(C) CÔTE DE BEAUNE – *continued*

Commune.	I Cuvée.	II Cuvée.	Area.
SAVIGNY-LES-BEAUNE		Aux Clous	38
		Aux Serpentières	12
		Aux Petits-Liards	15
		Aux Grands-Liards	16
		Es Canardises	26
		Les Pimentiers	41
		Les Rouvrettes	14
BEAUNE	LES FÈVES		11
	LES GRÈVES		79
	Les Marconnets		25
	Les Bressandes		46
	Les Cras		12
	Le Clos-de-la-Mousse		8
	Le Clos-des-Mouches		62
	Les Champs-Pimonts		41
	Les Aigrots		21
	Les Avaux		33
	Les Sizies		20
	Les Pertuisots		14
	Les Vignes-Franches		25
	Les Boucherottes		21
	Les Reversées		13
	Aux Coucherias		56
	Les Teurons		56
	Les Toussaints		16
	Les Cent-Vignes		58
	Les Perrières		8
	Les Montrevenots		22
	La Montée-Rouge		41
		Les Blanches-Fleurs	23
		Clos-du-Roi	46
		Les Beaux-Fougets	14
		Les Epenottes	34
		Les Tuvilains	22

(c) CÔTE DE BEAUNE – *continued*

Commune.	I Cuvée.	II Cuvée.	Area.
BEAUNE		En Belissand	12
POMMARD	LES RUGIENS-BAS		14
	Les Epenots		27
	Le Clos-Blanc		10
	Les Petits-Epenots		49
	Les Rugiens-Hauts		19
	Les Jarolières		8
	Les Pézerolles		16
	Les Sausilles		13
	Les Argillières		9
	Clos de la Commareine		10
	Les Charmots		13
	Les Arvelets		21
	Les Bertins		9
	Les Fremiers		12
	Les Poutures		11
	Les Chaponnières		8
VOLNAY	LES CAILLERETS		35
	Les Fremiets		16
	Les Champans		28
	Les Angles		12
	En Chevret		16
	Carelles-sous-la-Chapelle		9
	En l'Ormeau		11
	Les Mitans		10
	En Brouillards		17
	En Taille-Pieds		18
	La Robardelle		10
MONTHELIE	Les Champs-Fulliots		22
	La Taupine		4
	Le Cas Rougeot		1½
	Clos Gauthey		3½
AUXEY-LE-GRAND		Les Duresses	23
		Les Reugnes	8

(c) CÔTE DE BEAUNE – *continued*

Commune.	I *Cuvée.*	II *Cuvée.*	Area.
AUXEY-LE-GRAND		Les Grands-Champs	11
		Les Bretterins	6
		Les Ecusseaux	16
MERSAULT (Red)	LES SANTENOTS-DU-MILIEU		20
	Les Cras		12
	Les Pelures		27
		Les Criots	11
		Les Corbins	22
		En Luraule	8
		Le Cromin	23
		Le Clos-de-Mazerey	8
		Les Mieux-Chavaux	25
		Le Pré-de-Manche	9
MERSAULT (White)	LES PERRIÈRES		42
	Les Genevrières		41
	Les Charmes-Dessus		38
	Le Porusot-Dessus		17
	La Pièce-sous-le-Bois		27
		Les Charrons	47
		La Goutte-d'Or	14
		Les Chevalières	25
		Le Tesson	14
		Les Charmes-Dessous	30
PULIGNY-MONTRACHET (White)	LE MONTRACHET (*vide* Commune de Chassagne)		10

(c) CÔTE DE BEAUNE – *continued*

Commune.	I Cuvée.	II Cuvée.	Area.
PULIGNY-MONTRACHET			
(White)	Les Combettes		17
	Le Chevalier-Montrachet		15
	Le Bâtard-Montrachet		24
	(*vide* Commune de Chassagne)		
	Blagny-Blanc		11
	Champ-Canet		11
	Les Chalumeaux		18
		Les Referts	32
(Red)	Le Cailleret		13
		Le Clavoillon	14
		Les Pucelles	17
CHASSAGNE-MONTRACHET			
(White)	LE MONTRACHET		9
	Le Bâtard-Montrachet		31
(Red)	Clôs Saint-Jean		35
	La Boudriotte		44
	La Maltroie		23
	Les Brussanes		39
	Champgain		71
		Les Mazures	71
		Les Vergers	23
		Le Clos Devaut	45
		Les Chenevottes	28
		Les Macherelles	20
SANTENAY	Les Gravières		72
		En Boichot	32
		Le Clos Tavannes	

(c) CÔTE DE BEAUNE – *continued*

Commune.	I *Cuvée.*	II *Cuvée.*	*Area.*
SANTENAY		En Beauregard	84
		En Beaurepaire	43
		La Maladière	34
		Le Grand-Clos-Rousseau	47
		La Comme	80
		En Passe-Temps	31
		Les Prarons-Dessus	45

CHAPTER TWENTY

FRENCH WINES OTHER THAN CLARETS AND BURGUNDIES

(A) CHAMPAGNE

CHAMPAGNE is a blended wine made from grapes grown in the Arrondissements of Châlons, Epernay, and Reims, together with some communes of Vitry-le-François, in the Marne. It can be (against the current English conception) red, pink or white and sparkling or still. I remember drinking a delightful pink Veuve Cliquot at the Verdun, in Marseille, some years ago.

The following are the principal manufacturers of champagne.

Ayala, Billecart-Salmon, Binet Fils & Co., Charles de Cazanove, Veuve Cliquot-Ponsardin, Couvert, Delbeck & Co., Deutz & Geldermann, Duminy & Co., Charles Farre, Fréminet & Fils, George Goulet, Henry Goulet, Heidsieck & Co. Monopole, Charles Heidsieck, Ernest Irroy, Krug & Co., Lanson Père et Fils, Lecureux & Co., Moët & Chandon, Duc de Montebello, G. H. Mumm & Co., Perrier-Jouet & Co., Joseph Perrier Fils & Co., Piper-Heidsieck, Pol Roger & Co., Pommery & Greno, Ch. & A. Prieur, Renaudin-Bollinger & Co., Louis Roederer, Ruinart Père et Fils, De Saint-Marceaux & Co.

FRENCH WINES

(B) THE LOIRE

The wines of the Loire can be roughly divided into three categories – namely those of the upper Loire, those of Touraine and those of Anjou. The principal growths are as follows:

(1) CHANTELLE (red). Clos des Près-Gaillards.
Clos des Anches.
Clos des Rochelles.
Clos de Gizat.
(white) Pouilly-sur-Loire.
(2) TOURAINE Vouvray.
(white) Rochecorbon.
Montlouis.
Sainte-Redegonde.
Vernou.
(red) Joué.
Saint-Avertin.
Chinon.
Bourgeuil
(3) ANJOU. (*a*) Coteaux de Layon.
Bonnezeaux.
Beaulieu.
Quarts de Chaumes.
Rablay.
(*b*) Coteaux de la Loire.
La Coulée de Serrant.
La Roche aux Moines.
Savennières.
La Possonnière.
Ingrandes.
(*c*) Coteaux de Saumur.
Montsoreau.
Turquant.
Parnay.
Souzay.
Dampierre.

(c) ALSACE

Of the Alsace growths the following may be noted:

Molsheim, Wolxheim, Barr, Obernai, Guebwiller, Ernoldsheim, Saverne, Ribeauvillé, Riquewihr, Reppoltsweiler, Zahnacker, Trottacker, Thann, Turkheim, Ammerschwihr, Heiligenstein, Kiensheim.

(d) THE JURAS

Of the Jura wines, the following:

Arbois, Arsures, Poligny, Marznoz, Pupillin, Névy-sur-Seille, Port-Lesney, Lavigny, Vernantois, Conliège, Beaufort, Ménétru, Salins, Authume, Jouhe, Gredisans, Menotey, Rainans and Château-Châlon.

(e) SAVOY

Of the Savoy wines:

Talloires, Marignier, Saint-Jean-la-Porte, Coteau-Bard, Seyssel, Ayse, Montagneux, Chevelu, Marétel, Manicle, Virieu, Belmont, Vin des Altesses.

(f) THE RHÔNE

Of the wines grown in the Rhône valley, south of Lyon and the Beaujolais, may be noted the following, moving downstream:

Côte Rotie, Château Grillet (white), Hermitage (red and white) and the Châteauneuf-du-Papes, such as Château de Vaudieu, Domaine des Serres, Clos des Papes, Clos St.-Pierre, Vieux Télégraphe, etc.

(g) THE MIDI

Of the wines grown in the Midi – i.e. the departments of the Alpes-Maritimes, Var, Bouche-du-Rhône,

Gard, Hérault, and so forth, there is little to say. I, personally, have drunk a great number of these local growths without finding one of any distinction at all. Cassis (near Ciotat) is praised, but I have never liked it; and a Varois wine called Camp Romain is now much in evidence locally which I think even poorer. The vast vineyards between Montpellier and Narbonne (St.-Georges, etc.) produce the huge material out of which pseudo Bordeaux, Burgundy, etc., is manufactured. The only really agreeable wines (the sweet dessert wine of Frontignan excepted) I have found in the Midi come from Roussillon, in the Pyrénées Orientales.

THIRD PART
SQUATTING

CHAPTER TWENTY-ONE

THE ENGLISH COLONY

I DO not know when that quaint, if somewhat nebulous entity, the English Colony, such as we know it to-day, first took root in French soil. Perhaps it may be said to have begun with Lord Brougham, two years after the passing of the Reform Bill. Whenever and however this phenomenon was born, it has become in the course of nearly a century as acclimatised and accepted (if not as acceptable) as football matches, five o'clocks, briar pipes, Sunlight soap, billy-cock hats, Thomas Cook, cocktails and the jazz band.

The English Colony may be regarded as of two kinds – that of the workers and that of the workless. That is, of those who live in France because of their employment and of those who do so for pleasure, health, economy, or because they are not wanted (or, perhaps, are very particularly wanted) at home. The former type is of less interest (if of more use) than the latter: also it is comparatively small in numbers and is naturally confined to the large cities. In Marseille, for example, there is an English business colony quite apart from that of the gay, the idle, the egregious and the retired. The two do not mix. Nor do I propose to concern myself with the former type. They coalesce with their French colleagues: often intermarry with them, and, in general, 'go native.' They represent, of course, the English in France most worth knowing, but they are too busy to bother themselves with the tourist or the English colonists of the other kind, except in so far as their business necessitates such contact. The Englishman or American, proposing to reside in France, for health, pleasure or the other reasons enumerated above – either wholly or seasonally – is not likely to meet them. He will meet, however, many thousands in the same category as himself; for the whole of the southern littoral is so thickly plastered with English colonists, that a bottle of whisky could almost be passed from hand to hand without any native help, all the way from Menton to Marseille – but there would be precious little whisky in it by the time it got there.

In such a welter of what the French would call déracinés, it is natural that the would-be settler of taste and discretion should feel himself somewhat at a loss; first as to where to settle; and secondly, having done so, as to how to behave. Bear-gardens and monkey-houses are not always easy to live in, however pleasant and ubiquitous may be the buns and nuts; and any man of sense and sensibility will soon learn (if he has not guessed it already) that he will meet Englishmen (and women) abroad such as he never meets – and, possibly, will never want to meet – at home. But you cannot have your cake and eat it, and some price must be paid for climate and economy.

It should be borne in mind that a vast change has taken place in the English colony in Europe during the last twenty years. This change is as simple as abrupt, and can be expressed in a sentence. Before the war, the Englishman lived abroad because he could afford it: to-day he lives abroad because he cannot afford to live anywhere else — too often (for the good name of English credit) not even here. As M. Siegfried has but recently pointed out, the old French conception of the Englishman — gentle, urbane and generous — has wholly vanished, to be superseded by that of a man, blatant, mean and (to tell the truth) dishonest. I know of places in France where to be an Englishman is almost synonymous with R.D. upon a cheque. The blame is ours. I have watched this declension growing steeper over the last ten years. It is deplorable. For to live in a foreign country — especially if one does so of choice and not necessity — is to undertake a particular obligation. One is, *ipso facto*, in the honourable position of an ambassador, and one's behaviour should be, in all respects, conformable to such an appointment. For it is by the British resident among them that the French people learn to estimate the English — for the Frenchman travels little abroad and least of all in England, where the exchange is adverse to him.

Presidents and Ministers may know better, but it is the man in the street who, in the end, dictates foreign policy. One drunk in a café — one dud cheque to a grocer, may (indeed, will), in the long run, cause a deeper rift in the lute of peace than an extra battleship or another Army Corps. It is well that English visitors to France — and elsewhere for that matter — should be meticulous as to their behaviour.

The Gentle Traveller, however, will be in no need

of these admonitions; and should he wish to settle, temporarily or permanently, in France, he will only concern himself with unworthy colonists, in so far as to avoid being inculpated with them; and, according to this intention, his purse, his tastes and his health, he must decide where to live. If he wishes to settle where he can enjoy the society of his fellow-countrymen, his choice will be confined (Paris excepted) to, roughly, three littorals; namely, the coasts of Normandy and Brittany; the coast of Béarn and the Mediterranean coast. If he proposes to divide his year between England and France, he is more likely to choose the southern littoral as a winter residence; Béarn or Brittany as a summer one.

Although of a Norman family, I know little of Brittany or Normandy, having lived mostly in Provence. I believe one can live there very comfortably, and the food, of course, is famous. But its climate in winter is not appreciably better than that of England. The Bay of Biscay is mild enough in winter, but wet and windy. The Mediterranean is, on the whole, the best, despite the mistral.

If the would-be settler chooses the south (for climatic reasons he probably will), he must have a care of this same mistral – the bugbear of Provence. Legend has it that it comes out of a cave near Valence: it certainly begins to blow from about here down the Rhône valley with an increasing force, usually reaching its climax about Avignon. Near Aix-en-Provence it begins to split into two, one half blowing south-eastward and eastward as far as Cannes: the other half blowing south-westward and westward as far as

THE ENGLISH COLONY

Narbonne. It is a wind that blows in gusts, often of great intensity and is commonly said to last for three, six, or nine days. Its best (or worst) efforts occur generally in February and March. It is none the less a fine weather wind, and is an excellent scavenger. The English settler should see to it that his house is so placed as to be sheltered from this wind or built with its back to it. Old Provençal houses (Mas) are usually without windows on the mistral side.

I strongly urge the settler to call upon the English consul or vice-consul for his district as soon as convenient. This is not commonly practised by the English colonist who, as a rule, neglects the consul altogether until he needs him — when, sometimes, it is too late. Such a practice is not only discourteous, but unfair to the consul who is responsible for the well-being of his fellow-countrymen living in his area. Consuls are poorly paid and much harassed folk (most vice-consuls are unpaid), who are constantly being called upon to take up arms against a sea of other people's troubles. I remember the Vice-consul of X telling me of a dear old lady who called upon him (together with six little dogs) to negotiate a small loan. She explained that she had spent all her money shopping and had no money to return home. Money was offered for the tram fare, but this was negatived on account of the six little doggies who could not travel by tram. She left, at last, with a loan of fifty francs; but my friend was called up by the police next morning to bail out an elderly English lady who had been found dead to the world in the early hours of the morning in a quiet street, surrounded by six little lap-dogs.

If the settler chooses a small place to live in, as apart from the greater English colonies, such as Nice, Cannes, Monte Carlo, Biarritz and so forth – that is to say, if he lives in a part more peculiarly French, he should place himself en rapport with the priest of his parish. If he be fidèle, he will, of course, be of his flock; but whatever his religion, or lack of religion, may be, it is, again, only courteous for the stranger to acknowledge the priest of his parish. The curés in the country in France are deserving, as a whole, of the greatest affection and respect. They know their parishes as few English clergymen (I fear) know theirs; and although the church has long been disestablished in France, the curé has more real power than a dozen mayors or a hundred policemen. There is no harm, however, in standing the policeman a drink or the mayor a dinner as well – and, of course, separately.

If the settler chooses to install himself in one of the big towns, he will find himself as much at home (as regards his surroundings) as in England. He will have, at hand, the English club, the English doctor, the English clergyman, the English library, the English chemist, grocer, and so forth, and can imagine himself at Bournemouth, Brighton, Bexhill, Torquay or Tunbridge Wells as his mood and humour take him. The smaller places are cheaper and more entertaining, but the English resident will have to deal to some extent directly with the native, and to bear in mind that his compatriots in these remoter parts are there for a variety of reasons, not always in respect to a love of retirement or the need for rest or quiet. He will, therefore, be as cautious as compassionate. If he be of an independent spirit, and wishful to escape the boredom and evade the perils of an English colony, he may seek a habitation in native areas, as yet untouched by the Nordic pioneer. Provided he knows enough of the vernacular to understand and be understood and has, moreover, some degree of adaptation to the native way of life, there is no reason why he should not do this — always supposing he can break into virgin ground. In the hinterland, this is easy enough; for the coastal settlements rarely penetrate more than a dozen miles or so from the sea. And he can do so at a fraction of the cost he would incur within the settled areas — even in the Var or the Alpes-Maritimes. But then, practically speaking, the coast-line is the only livable part of Provence. One might live for years in places like Draguignan, Manosque, Aups, Coursegoules, Puget-Theniers, etc., without meeting another English resident — if one did not die in the meantime; for no man of sense would live in these places unless the care of property held him there or he was anxious not to be found out. About the only bearable inland town in Provence is Aix and that is already as full of English as a dog is of fleas. I doubt if there is a village on all the sea-board of the Alpes-Maritimes and the Var (not to mention Béarn) that has not its quota of English settlers, with the possible exception of one or two places peculiarly invested by the international sweepings of Montparnasse. To the west of Marseille, to be sure, there is more chance for the adventurous pioneer. But the coast here is flat and malarial — the small strip between l'Estaque and the Port du Bouc excepted — and the climate of Languedoc as a whole is vile,

STILL LIFE IN AIX-EN-PROVENCE

being grillingly hot in summer and bitterly cold in winter.

An Englishman willing to forgo the evident merits (and demerits) of the Riviera, and anxious to acquaint himself with the best of French provincial life, might be advised to settle in one of the more salubrious central departments, such as the Nièvre or the Yonne, or westward in the Angoumois or Poitou. In these parts, he will be able to escape his compatriots – for the which he does not presumably go to France to meet – and may even hope to encounter real Frenchmen; and least, he will hear better French spoken than in Nice or Marseille.

That he will get to know the French around him will depend upon himself and his introductions. Without the latter, unless he is happily able to render some service, he may, perhaps, be asked out to a formal luncheon party after a number of years of residence. Do not blame the French too much in this. Remember that a Frenchman might live for half a lifetime in the Dukeries, lacking introduction, without so much as tossing off a gin and bitters with a single Duke. The French are, at heart, a kindly, genuine and even hospitable people, but they do not invite you into their families until they know you.

Nor, indeed, do the English.

CHAPTER TWENTY-TWO

DOMESTIC ECONOMY

The Perfect Socialist State having not yet arrived, man has, unhappily, still need of money in an imperfect world. One still has to pay one's rent – or its equivalent in interest. The butcher and the baker expect to be paid – sometime. Heat, light, and water are not given away to deserving, or even undeserving, citizens. All of which is a great pity, but cannot, I suppose, be helped. There may be excuse, therefore, for a brief note as to the cost of living to the settler in France. For unless he be of the class that live by what economists call the champagne standard, he will have some care – in many cases an urgent need – for domestic economy. Especially since the majority of English who decide to live in France, do so, at least in part, upon an economic urge. For such as can afford to rent luxury villas in Cannes or Antibes and so forth, these figures are not written.

Sir Walter Layton, the editor of the *Economist*, has recently pointed out that the ratio between the average wages of a French workman and that of an English workman is as three to five. I think it might be fairly said that the cost of living in France of the higher bourgeois standard as compared to that in England is at about the same ratio. That is to say, taking it by and large, for an annual expenditure of say from £500 to £1000, it is 40 per cent. cheaper to live in France than in England: the caveat being made, of course, as to excepting all places that have become Anglicised and have therefore adopted an English economic index. The cost of living varies widely in France itself, just as in England — the country being cheaper than the town: inland, as a rule, than the sea-board. Paris is cheaper than London — probably by much more than the three-five ratio. But I do not propose to touch on the Parisian problem here. Of the three Riviera capitals, Monte Carlo is undoubtedly the cheapest to live in: Nice, the next, and Cannes the most expensive. Comfortable flats can be found in Monte Carlo at under 12,000 francs or £100 a year. Commodities are, on the other hand, costly, and service both dear and difficult. Anywhere on the littoral is naturally more expensive than in the hinterland. If one can still discover a seaside village on these coasts unaffected by an English colonisation — which tends to raise rentals and wages by 100 per cent. and commodities by 30 per cent., the following figures may give some rough indication of costs.

A small villa of about six to eight rooms, kitchen, bath, etc., garage and garden — in an accessible position, with electric light and company's water — unfurnished or skeleton furnished — should not be more than 6000 francs or £50 a year on a short lease; less, of course, on a long one. The usual practice in France for short leases is a 3–6–9 years' lease, the renewal being at the option of the lessee. It may be pointed out that a landlord in France has great difficulty in evicting a tenant, even when his lease has expired. In effect, the landlord is under legal obligation to find a new habitation for his tenant equal in cost and convenience to his former one. As the tenant can always plead the unsuitability of other properties available at the same price, the only way the landlord can turn him out is to prove him undesirable as a tenant.

If we presume a villa of the size indicated above and a family of two occupying it, what is called in France a 'bonne à tout faire' is all the service necessary for the house. She should also do the washing; although, except in country districts, this is not easy to arrange. English infiltration and proletarian ideal have debauched good service in most places. The French bourgeois would not pay in wages more than about 200 francs a month or £20 per annum: 250 to 300 francs would be expected of the English. It is the custom to include vin ordinaire for the bonne in these wages. She would expect a litre a day, at a price of about two francs a litre. General living expenses (drinks excepted) should for two people and the bonne come to not more than about £3 a week – for an ordinary good cuisine bourgeoise. It is not easy to find a vin ordinaire of a superior quality in France to-day at much under 5 francs a litre – although this price varies according to the district and the palate of the drinker. Nothing (or anything) may be spent on the cellar, but assuming a modest consumption of crus bourgeois, one may fairly add a weekly drink bill of another £1 a week – if the apéro' is strictly confined to French brands. Addiction to gins and bitters, whiskies and soda and so forth naturally swells the drink bill to an alarming extent.

The cost of electricity (light only) for a villa of, say, 30 points should not exceed £5 to £7 a year – again according to the district. Water may be put at another £5 per annum, unless one is a gardening fan or a bath maniac. Heating, in small houses in the country, is usually by stoves burning wood or briquettes. Cooking – in summer – is often done by charcoal. It is difficult to estimate fuel costs. But one may put an approximate figure at £10 per annum.

Local (municipal) taxes in France are in small places slight – probably not more than 50 to 100 francs a year. If a reasonable insurance rate be included, one may put the house expenses – i.e. rent, heat, light, water, taxes and insurance – for a villa, as indicated, at about £80 per annum. Thus, if we take wages (say) at £30 and living (food and wine) expenses at about £4 a week, the total yearly budget should stand at about £310 – all personal and accidental expenses, travel, car and so forth, of course excepted. One item is still to be added – namely, French income-tax. Any foreigner is taxed who:

(*a*) Holds property (lease or free-hold) in France.
(*b*) Lives habitually in France – even in hotels, etc. Habitual residence is taken to be one year or periods amounting to one year.

A foreign resident thus liable to income-tax is not required to declare his income, but is assessed for tax at an assumed income of seven times the rent he pays. Thus, in the above case, where the rent paid is 6000 francs per annum, the tenant would be assessed on an income of 42,000 francs or about £350 per annum. The scale of French income-tax is a sliding one and somewhat complicated: it is given in Appendix B. In this particular case, assuming a married couple (over two years married and childless) the income-tax would amount to about 770 francs or some £6.

Foreign residents in France are also required to take out a carte d'identité, which costs 100 francs for two years. Certain reductions are made for students, men of letters belonging to accredited societies and so forth. We may therefore assume the total living expenses of the couple occupying this hypothetical villa to be about £320 a year, inclusive of all taxes. This figure might be sensibly reduced by residence in the remoter parts of the interior and very greatly exceeded in the urban or suburban areas of places such as Nice, Cannes or Biarritz.

The income-tax by the way, is paid (in person) at the office of the 'perception' in the resident's town or district. The tenant will probably not be called upon to make a declaration, the detail or rental being supplied to the office by the landlord.

The settler in a rural area will certainly wish to keep a car. A few notes as to the procedure to be adopted may be of use.

The owner of a car (of French registration) in France has to possess at least two documents – three, if he wishes to drive himself. These are, first, the Carte Grise. This card is obtained on the purchase of the car, and has to be taken out for it at the local Préfecture. This card bears the registered number of the car and the owner's name and address, and must be surrendered when the car is sold. It may take a day or two to obtain the Carte Grise, in which case a temporary card and number (a 'W.W.' number) is issued forthwith to the purchaser by the agent from whom he buys the car. Secondly, there is the permis de circulation, which is issued by the local office of the contributions indirectes upon payment of the car tax. It is, in effect, a receipt for the tax, which may be paid either quarterly or half-yearly – but not for a period under three months. Thirdly, no one can drive a car in France without possessing a permis de conduire or Carte Rose. To obtain this, one has to undergo a test by an official of the Ministry of Mines – though why this department so concerns itself has always been a mystery to me. Application must be made (on stamped paper – 3 frs. 50) to the Préfecture for a 'convocation.' This, owing to press of applications, usually takes some weeks to obtain. One is then tested by the Inspector, as to driving, traffic regulations and general care of the car. They commonly ask what you would do if the car caught fire – the desired answer being, to turn off the petrol. In my own examination I fear I replied, 'Let the car burn out and claim full insurance for a new one.' They passed me all the same. A photo is needed for the Carte Rose. The law also demands that the car owner should have his name engraved, as also his address, in metal, fixed, in a visible position (usually on the dashboard) in the car. He is liable to be stopped at any time by the police to show his three cards; namely, the Carte Rose, the Carte Grise and the Permis de Circulation. The Carte Grise lasts for the life of the car – the Carte Rose for the life of the driver – unless it is cancelled for bad driving, etc.

Owners of French registered cars wishing to travel outside France, must possess themselves of:

(*a*) Carnet de Passages en Douanes.
(*b*) Certificat International pour Automobiles.
(*c*) Permis International de Conduire.

It must be borne in mind, what is not usually known, that non-nationals driving French cars cannot use the 'passavant' in their Carnet de Passages, but must obtain a separate 'passavant' at the first frontier they intend to cross. This document is only issued by the frontier office and lasts (as do the other documents) for one year. It has to be endorsed every time the car leaves or enters France.

As to the cost of a car in France, petrol is dearer than in England, but the taxation on the car is less. Petrol varies in price from the lower grades at 8 francs a 'bidon' to 'Esso' (Ethyl) at about 13. Energic (B.P.) can usually be bought for 9. A bidon is five litres or 1.1 gallons. High-grade oil costs about 22 francs per 2 litres. Thus petrol may be said to average 1s. 6d. a gallon; oil, 2s. a quart. A table of car taxes is given in Appendix C. It should be noted that the French horse power is different from the English 'R.A.C.' rating. For example a 13 c.v. (French) car would be rated in England for tax purposes at 18 h.p. In France, if a car is not used but stored in a garage, tax exemption can be claimed for the period of such storage (over a certain minimum) upon the affidavit of the garage proprietor that the car has not left the garage. If a chauffeur is employed, his wages (in the country) should not exceed 900 francs a month – the man living out; that is to say, about 37s. 6d. a week.

One word might be added as to the evasion by residents abroad of English income-tax. A great number

DOMESTIC ECONOMY

of English people live in France (and Italy) with the not very laudable purpose of escaping their own national taxation. To be frank, I have small sympathy with these tax-dodgers. It is all very well for the rentier class in England to grumble at heavy taxation, but they are paying this in support of their 'rents.' That is to say, we are paying 4s. 6d. in the £1 in order to keep the £1 at par value. Taxation (and unemployment) are the direct price we pay for deflation. In France, where the franc was inflated to a fifth its value, the rentier class were practically ruined. It is plainly more advantageous to have £1000 a year and pay £225 a year in income-tax than to have £200 a year and pay £2 a year tax. This is not economics: it is simple arithmetic. No, I have no use for the tax-dodgers. Nor is this exercise as easy as it sounds. Many people have quite erroneous ideas as to this, and as a warning and deterrent to English people hoping to escape their obligations in this way, I may point out that

(a) Rebate for foreign residents is only allowed where such residence is a bona fide one: that is, where only a minimum time is spent in England and the claimant has no residence at all in England.

(b) Acceptance or refusal of such claim is entirely within the discretion of the Commissioners.

(c) Such claims can only be admitted upon
   (1) Income from investments outside England.
   (2) Government pensions.
   (3) Moneys earned outside England: e.g. salaries earned in France, royalties accruing from American copyrights and so forth.

I do not say that one is not justified in availing oneself

of the privilege that the law of one's country allows one; and for the bona fide resident, *in partibus infidelium*, not to do so, would be, perhaps, to be hypochondriacally conscientious. But I do say that the sight of hordes of the English middle class dashing to France and Italy for the sole purpose of dodging income-tax is, to put it mildly, scarcely an exhilarating spectacle.

CHAPTER TWENTY-THREE

ADMONITION

'THE learned SMELFUNGUS,' wrote the Best of Travellers, 'travelled from Boulogne to Paris – from Paris to Rome – and so on – but he set out with spleen and jaundice, and every object he passed by was discoloured or distorted – He wrote an account of them, but 'twas nothing but the account of his miserable feelings.'

This was said by Sterne of Smollet and might still be said of too many Englishmen, travelling in Europe to-day. So perhaps some excuse may be made for appending herewith some admonitory notes, to the elimination of that spleen and jaundice, which but destroys the benefits of foreign travel. That entertaining little book, *Brighter French*, is described as an attempt to make one think as a Frenchman thinks.

No advice to the traveller could be better than this; so:

(1) Try to think as a Frenchman thinks; or at least, try to think how he thinks.

(2) Remember that France was possessed of a culture and a civilisation when we had none.

(3) Remember that France still regards itself as the one custodian of *La Finesse* (this word is untranslatable).

(4) Remember that a Frenchman or Frenchwoman regards an Englishman, au fond, as a barbarian.

(5) Be careful not to give occasion for such belief.

(6) Remember that to be drunk in France is not considered witty – only boorish.

(7) Bear in mind that French is, probably, the most elegant spoken language in the world. Do not murder it more than you can help.

(8) Remember that more Englishmen talk about cold baths than ever take them.

(9) Remember that when you are spending ten francs, the Frenchman has to spend the equivalent to him of fifty. The luck of the exchange is with you, but you need not make a song about it.

(10) Remember that the gay life of Paris is staged almost entirely for the Americans, the English and the Germans; and that the morality of an English country town would shock a French country town into voluntary excommunication.

(11) Do not judge the French by the people you meet. As a tourist you will meet little but the hôtellerie, who for the most part, are not French.

(12) Do not demand whisky, gin, beefsteak, chops, tomato sauce and so on, except in places given over to the English. These may be all very well in their way, but one does not, presumably, travel to France to enjoy them.

(13) As a set-off, ask any travelled Frenchman what he thinks of English hotel food.

(14) Do not suppose that, because you are English, you are, *ipso facto*, going to be swindled. There are scamps in all countries, and to expect to be swindled is but to invite it.

(15) Remember that customs officials, policemen

and the like, have a thankless task to perform. The surest way of receiving courtesy is to tender it.

(16) Parade-ground manners are not well received in France – especially from a foreigner. You would not dare to use them at home; so don't advertise them abroad.

(17) The Frenchman shakes hands and removes his hat more often than we do. He will not necessarily expect the same of you, but a little formal politeness does no harm.

(18) The motorist should remember not to cut or double around corners. The French driver considers he can take a corner at the highest speed he is capable of, as long as he keeps to his own side; as, legally, he is entitled to do. The driver who drives in France disregarding the laws of the road will not live long.

(19) Remember that what is technically called 'audible warning of approach' is expected in France, not discouraged as in England. You are under obligation to sound your horn at all cross roads and where visibility is lacking, and to answer when a horn is sounded. This precaution is not considered 'bad form' in France.

(20) Remember, in general, that in France, you are expected to be no longer a schoolboy, but grown up and able to look after yourself. Nobody else will do it for you, anyhow.

APPENDICES

APPENDIX (A)

The following is a list of restaurants in the provinces, starred (gastronomically) in Michelin (1931). The larger towns – e.g. Marseille, Lyon, etc. – have been omitted; as also a few places, starred in Michelin, but which I cannot conscientiously recommend from personal experience. Where two or more houses in any particular town are starred in Michelin, the one cited herewith is that which is known to M. Cousin or myself: or, failing this, that which is best spoken of by the 'Club-sans-Club.'

It should be borne in mind that M. Cousin has, so far, only published three books dealing with, roughly:

(*a*) Paris and the neighbouring departments: e.g. Seine, Seine-et-Oise, Seine-et-Marne, Oise, Eure, Calvados, etc.

(*b*) Provence, the Dauphiné and Savoy.

(*c*) Languedoc and Gascony,

whilst the present volume is necessarily limited to the itineraries therein specified. Houses recommended by M. Cousin or myself or both are herewith printed in heavier type.

TOWN	HOUSE
NORD	
Bailleul	Épée de Blé
Bavai	Café de Paris

APPENDIX A

TOWN	HOUSE
NORD – *continued*	
Cambrai	Taverne
Caudry	Europe
Fourmies	Providence
Hautemont	Gare
Douai	Boussard
Dunkerque	Trassaert
Estaires	Marchault-Lefebvre
Roubaix	Univers
Tourcoing	Café Moderne
Trélon	Commerce
Valenciennes	Rocher Cancale
PAS-DE-CALAIS	
Ardres	Coolen
Boulogne-sur Mer	Liégeoise
Calais	Trois Suisses
Hesdin	France
Liévin	Voyageurs
SEINE-INFÉRIEURE	
la Bouille	St.-Pierre
Caudebec-en-Caux	Marine
Duclair	Poste
Elbeuf	Grand Hôtel
Fécamp	Deux Aubépines
Forges-les-Eaux	Casino
le Havre	Grosse Tonne
Luneray	Cheval Blanc
Rouen	Couronne
St.-Valery-en-Caux	Hennetier
le Tréport	Filet-de-Sole
Totes	Cygne
Val de la Haye	Méridien
SOMME	
Abbeville	Roux
Amiens	Godbert
le Crotoy	Bonne Maman
Mers-les-Bains	Lutetia

APPENDIX A

TOWN	HOUSE
SOMME – *continued*	
Montdidier	Commerce
OISE	
Beauvais	Châteaubriand
Breteuil-sur-Noye	Globe
Compiègne	Royal Lieu
Ermenonville	Jean-Jacques
Lamorlaye	Host du Lys.
Mouy	Café de l'Hôtel Français
Noyon	Alliés
Pont-Ste-Maxence	Café Commerce
St.-Just-en-Chaussée	**St.-Nicolas**
Senlis	Gargantua
Vieux-Moulin	Mon St.-Pierre
Vivier-Frère-Robert	Clos Normand
ARDENNES	
Charleville-Mézières	Buffet de la Gare
Rethel	Sanglier des Ardennes
AISNE	
Château Thierry	Jean de la Fontaine
Liesse	Trois Rois
le Nouvion-en-Thiérache	Pétion
MEURTHE-ET-MOSELLE	
Nancy	Stanislas
MEUSE	
Ligny-en-Barrois	Cheval Blanc
Montmédy	Rose
Revigny-sur-Ornain	Est
Romagne-sous-Montfaucon	Café Français
St.-Mihiel	Rollot
Verdun	St.-Airy
MARNE	
Châlons-sur-Marne	Haute Mère Dieu
Dormans	Sourdet
Épernay	Chapon Fin
Sézanne	France
Vienne-le-Château	Host. Argonne

APPENDIX A

TOWN	HOUSE
SEINE-ET-MARNE	
Chaumes-en-Brie	Pont de l'Yères
Chennevières-sur-Marne	Ecu de France
Claye-Souilly	Touristes
Coubert	Écureuil
Crouy-sur-Ourcq	Écu
Dampmard	Quincangrogne
la Ferté-sous-Jouarre	Epée
Germigny-l'Évêque	Auberge de Germigny
Lagny	Moulin Bleu
Melun	**Université**
Montigny-sur-Loing	**Vanne Rouge**
Moret-sur-Loing	**Pallet**
Nemours	Rocher de Pierre le Sault
Ozoir-la-Ferrière	Coq Faisan
Ponthierry	Relais Galant
Souppes	Mouton
Thomery	Fours-du-Roi
SEINE	
Boulogne-Billancourt	Select
Choisy-le-Roi	Pompadour
la Garenne-Colombes	Pâtisserie Rose
Neuilly-sur-Seine	Host. de Neuilly
St.-Denis	Grand Cerf
Varenne-St.-Hilaire	Pavillon Bleu
Vincennes	**Cygne**
SEINE-ET-OISE	
Argenteuil	Rodelet
Auvers-sur-Oise	**Nord**
Boissy-St.-Leger	Tourne-Bride
Bonnières-sur-Soine	Terminus
Bougial	**Coq-Hardi**
Carrières-sur-Poissy	**Paul**
la Celle-St.-Cloud	Lys de la Vallée
Chanteloup-les-Vignees	Hermitage
Conflans-Ste.-Honorine	Fins Gourmets
Enghien-les-Bains	Terminus

APPENDIX A

TOWN	HOUSE
SEINE-ET-OISE — *continued*	
Houdan	Tasserie
Juziere	Goujon-Folichon
Dampierre	**Auberge St.-Pierre**
Deunemont	Roi René
Essonnes	Hermitage
Etampes	Grand Monarque
l'Isle-Adam	Écu de France
Maison Laffitte	**Charmattes**
Marines	**Paris**
Maule	Petit Quinquin
Meulon	Grande Pinte
Corbeil	Pantrat
St-Remy-l'Honore	Moulin de Bicherel
Cernay-la-Ville	Léopold
Mézières	Fontaine
Montlignon	Bouquet de la Vallée
Montmorency	Pavillon de Flore
Orgeval	Moulin d'Orgeval
Orsay	**Latour**
Palaiseau	**Moulin de la Planche**
le Perray	Forêt Verte
Queue-les-Yvelines	Auberge des Yvelines
Rosny-sur-Seine	**Vert-Galant**
Poissy	**Esturgeon**
Pontoise	Vieux Manoir
Rambouillet	**De la Garenne**
la Roche-Guyon	Au Vieux Donjon
Rolleboise	**De la Corniche**
Reuil-Malmaison	Giquel
St.-Cloud	Garden Hotel
St.-Ouen-l'Aumône	Demi-Lune
St.-Remy-les-Chevreuse	Vallée
St.-Lambert-des-Bois	**Bonne Accueil**
Sèvres	Pêche Miraculeuse
Tessancourt	Closerie-des-Saules
Triel	**Marine**

APPENDIX A

TOWN	HOUSE
SEINE-ET-OISE – *continued*	
Vaucresson	Coq d'Or
Varenne-Jarcy	Moulin Jarcy
Vaux-sur-Seine	Coccinelle
Ville-d'Avray	Chaumière
EURE	
les Andelys	Grand Cerf
Beaumont-le-Roger	Lion d'Or
Evreux	Grand Cerf
Ezy	Corbeau
Neubourg	Beuvron
Nonancourt	Normandy
Pacy-sur-Eure	de la Gare
Pont-Audemer	Auberge du Vieux-Puits
la Rivière-Thibouville	Soleil d'Or
Tillières-sur-Avre	Bois Joly
Vernon	La Tour de Claire
ORNE	
Alençon	La Rotonde
Bagnoles-de-l'Orne	Charmettes
Ferté-Macé	Grand Turc
Domfront	Crémaillère
Fleurs	Rivet
Laigle	Café du Centre
le Mêle-sur-Sarthe	Chalottière
Sées	Gagneux
Tourouvre	France
Tubœuf	Auberge Épine
CALVADOS	
Bayeux	Ville de Bayeaux
Cabourg	Gente Arlette
Caen	Chandivert
Clécy	Moulin
Condé-sur-Noireau	Lion d'Or
Grandchamp-les-Bains	Grand
Dives-sur-Mer	Guillaume-le-Conquérant
Honfleur	Parisien
Lisieux	Coup d'Or

APPENDIX A

TOWN	HOUSE
CALVADOS – *continued*	
Luc-sur-Mer	Plage
Ouistrehain	Parc aux Huîtres
Pont-l'Évêque	Aigle d'Or
St.-Pierre-sur-Dives	Terrasse
Trouville	Maison Normande
Villers-sur-Mer	Paris-et-Plage
Villerville	Parisien
Vire	**Cheval Blanc**
MANCHE	
Avranches	Bonneau
Barfleur	Moderne
Grandville	Gourmet
Kairon-sur-Mer	Toque Blanche
Cherbourg	Grand Balcon
Mortain	Poste
Sourdeval	Commerce
Villedieu-les-Poëles	Louvre
Pontaubault	Gare
Quettehou	Commerce
FINISTÈRE	
Brest	Moderne
Châteaulain	Grande Maison
Châteauneuf-du-Faou	Belle Vue
Landivisiau	Commerce
Morlaix	Europe
Primel-Tregastel	Limbour
Quimper	Relais-St.-Corentin
Quimperlé	Vieille Maison
Riec-sur-Belon	Rouat
St.-Guénolé	Mogneron
Sizun	Mère Grall
CÔTE-DU-NORD	
Cap Fréhel	Fauconnière
Guingamp	Commerce
Dinan	Poste
Paimpol	Le Barbue

TOWN	HOUSE
CÔTE-DU-NORD – *continued*	
Pontrieux	Pommelet
St.-Brieuc	Commerce
Trégastel	Quo Vadis
le Val André	Chalet
MORBIHAN	
Fanet	Croix d'Or
Lorient	Terminus
Questembert	Bretagne
Rochebernard	Voyageurs
Rochefort-en-Terre	le Cadre
Trinité-sur-Mer	Voyageurs
ILLE-ET-VILAINE	
Fourgère	Voyageurs
Chenonceaux	Touristes
Pontréan	Boguais
Rennes	Armenonville
Rotheneuf	Rochers Sculptés
St.-Briac	Centre
MAYENNE	
Javron	Moderne
Laval	Continental
Mayenne	Croix Couverte
SARTHE	
la Ferté-Bernard	Château Rouge
la Flèche	Image
Fresney-sur-Sarthe	Ronsin
Sablé-sur-Sarthe	St.-Martin
St.-Mars-la-Brière	Chapeau Rouge
St.-Denis-d'Orques	Croissant
Chartre-sur-le-Loir	Cheval Blanc
Vibraye	Chapeau Rouge
EURE-ET-LOIR	
Châteaudun	**Host. Château**
Fermaincourt	Biche-au-Bois
Chartres	Pâtisserie Berthier
Illiers	Bourgneuf

APPENDIX A

TOWN	HOUSE
EURE-ET-LOIR – *continued*	
Jouy	Providence
Maintenant	Chaumière-et-Mamert
Sorel-Moussel	Val de l'Eure
LOIRET	
Beaugency	Écu de Bretagne
Briare	Petit Pompadour
la Chapelle-St.-Mesmin	Bellevue
Gien	Rivage de la Loire
Meung-sur-Loire	St.-Jacques
Nogent-sur-Vernisson	Puy-de-Dôme
Sully-sur-Loire	Poste
YONNE	
Auxerre	Tour d'Orbandelle
Chablis	Étoile
Joigny	Escargot
Quarré-les-Tombes	Nord
St.-Fargeau	Lion d'Or
St.-Valérien	Gatinais
Sens	Paris
Tonnerre	Buffet de la Gare
Toucy	Lion d'Or
AUBE	
Trainel	Cheval Blanc
Troyes	Buffet de la Gare
HAUTE-MARNE	
Bourbonne-les-Bains	Grand
VOSGES	
Contrexéville	Cosmos Palace
Eloiyes	Voyageurs
Épinal	Auberge d'Éloyes
BELFORT	
Belfort	Comète
HAUTE-SAÔNE	
Vesoul	Buffet de la Gare
CÔTE-D'OR	
Arnay-le-Duc	Terminus

APPENDIX A

TOWN	HOUSE
CÔTE-D'OR – *continued*	
Aisey-sur-Seine	Roi
Beaune	Poste
Châtillon-sur-Seine	Pavillon Bleu
les Laumes	Gare
Mersault	Chevreuil
Nolay	Ste.-Marie
Nuits-St.-Georges	Côte-d'Or
Pouilly-en-Auxois	Poste
Saulieu	Poste
Sémur-en-Auxois	Gourmets
NIÈVRE	
Châtillon-en-Bazots	France
Cercy-la-Tour	Commerce
Charité-sur-Loire	Terminus
Cosne	Tivoli
Lormes	Poste
Moulins-Englebert	Bon Laboureur
Nevers	Paix
Neuvy-sur-Loire	Paix
Prémery	Poste
St.-Honoré-les-Bains	Hardy
St.-Pierre-le-Moutier	Commerce
St.-Saulge	Poste
les Settons	Beau Rivage
CHER	
Aubigny-sur-Nère	Chaumière
Blet	France
Brisson-sur-Sauldre	Écu
Mehun-sur-Yèvre	Croix Blanche
St.-Florent-sur-Cher	Commerce
St.-Thibault	Étoile
Sancerre	Point-de-Jour
Sancoins	St.-Joseph
LOIR-ET-CHER	
Blois	Porc Epic
Chouzy-sur-Cesse	Relais d'Auteuil

APPENDIX A

TOWN	HOUSE
LOIR-ET-CHER — *continued*	
Montrichard	Croix Blanche
Motte-Beuvron	Grand Monarque
Vendôme	Paix
INDRE-ET-LOIRE	
Amboise	du Mail
Azay-le-Rideau	Commerce
Bléré	Commerce
Chinon	Vers Luisant
Cinq-Mars-la-Pile	Nord
la Haye-Descartes	Vieux Logis
Langeais	Maison de Rabelais
Ligueil	Poste
Loches	Palais
Preuilly-sur-Claise	Image et Promenade Réunis
Semblancy	Luxembourg
Tours	Lyonnais
Vouvray	Pont de Cisse
MAINE-ET-LOIRE	
Angers	Vert d'Eau
Baugé	Boule d'Or
Doué	Boule d'Or
Gennes	Loire
Ingrandes	Lion d'Or
Lion d'Angers	Voyageurs
Rosiers-sur-Loire	Ducs d'Anjou
St.-Florent-le-Vieil	Boule d'Or
St.-Georges-sur-Loire	Tête-Noire
Saumar	**Budan**
LOIRE-INFÉRIEURE	
Ancenis	Voyageurs
la Baule	Trois Faisans
Derval	Voyageurs
Herbignac	Voyageurs
Guérande	Princes
Nozay	Pélican
Nantes	Brasserie Moderne

APPENDIX A

TOWN	HOUSE
VENDÉE	
Chantonnay	Mouton
Roche-sur-Yonne	Europe
les-Sables-d'Olonne	Commerce
Ste.-Hermine	Voyageurs
DEUX-SÈVRES	
La Crèche	Gare
Parthenay	Buffet de la Gare
Sauze-Vaussais	Cygne
Thouars	Abélard
VIENNE	
Châtellerault	France
Chaunay	Central
Lussac-le-Château	Desjacques
Loudun	Papuchon
Montmorillon	Europe
Roche-Posay	Central
Poitiers	**Chapon Fin**
St.-Saviol	Gare
INDRE	
Argenton-sur-Creuse	Host. des Cordeliers
Châteauroux	Bijotat
St.-Benoît-du-Sault	Trois Cents Couverts
Valencay	Espagne
ALLIER	
Ferrières-sur-Sichon	Central
Gannat	Agriculture
Dompièrre-sur-Besbre	Commerce
Marcillat	Grand Hotel
Montlucon	Union
Néris-les-Bains	Grand
Moulins	Poulet
St.-Gérard-le-Puy	Paix
St.-Pourçain-sur-Sioule	Chêne-Vert
Vichy	Chanteclerc
SAÔNE-ET-LOIRE	
Autun	St.-Louis et Poste

APPENDIX A

TOWN	HOUSE
SAÔNE-ET-LOIRE – *continued*	
Chalon-sur-Saône	Bec Fin
Chagny	Commerce
Louhans	Commerce
Mâcon	**Larmatine**
Pontaneveaux	Compagnons de Jéhu
Paray-le-Monial	Terminus
JURA	
Baume-les-Messieurs	Belvedere
Champagnole	Grand Hotel
Clairvaux	Ethevenard
Doucier	Lamy
Lajoux	Haute Montagne
Lons-le-Saunier	Cheval Rouge
Morez	Central Moderne
Arbois	Marle
DOUBS	
Besançon	Palais du Gourmet
Malbuisson	Lac et Beausite
Nans-sous-Ste.-Anne	Perraud-Baudin
Ornans	France
Mouthier	Manoir
HAUTE-SAVOIE	
Annecy	**Brachon**
Amphion	Plage
Argentière	**Couronne**
Chamonix	Gourmets
Combloux	**P. L. M. du Mont Blanc**
Houches	Pont Ste.-Marie
Chavoire	**Ermitage**
la Clusaz	Lion d'Or
Douvaine	Poste
Evian-les-Bains	Brasserie Helvetia
Megève	Trois Pigeons
Monnetier-Mornex	Château de Monnetier
Menthon	Palace
Montriond	Lac

APPENDIX A

TOWN	HOUSE
HAUTE-SAVOIE – *continued*	
Morzine	Alpes
Pont-de-L'Abîme	Pont de l'Abîme
St.-Félix	Platanes
St.-Gervais-les-Bains	Cortena
St.-Julien-en-Genèvois	**Cheval Blanc**
Servoz	Cascades
Sallanche	**Chaumière**
Thonon-les-Bains	Corniche
Talloires	**Georges Bise**
Vallorcine	Mont Blanc
AIN	
Artemare	Berrard
Belley	**Pernolet**
Bourg-en-Bresse	Europe
Ceignes	Moulin-Chabaud
Fère-en-Tardenois	Comédie
Guise	Couronne
Châtillon-de-Michailie	Gonnet-Ballet
Lagnieu	**Fontaine d'Or**
Nantua	France
.Pérouges	Vieux Pérouges
Pont-de-Veyle	Samaine
Priay	**Bourgeois**
St.-Germain-de-Joux	Reygrobellet
Thoiry	XXe Siècle
Trévoux	Germain
Villars-les-Dombes	Dombes
Virieu-le-Grand	Voyageur
Vonnas	Blanc
RHÔNE	
Chessy	Val d'Azergues
Condrieu	Beau Rivage
les Halles	**Charreton**
Thizy	Laffay
Yzeron	Berger
Villefranche	**La Benoîte**

APPENDIX A

TOWN	HOUSE
LOIRE	
Andrézieux	Richard
Boën-sur-Lignon	Central
Charlieu	Reine Pédauque
Feurs	Parc et Provence
Roanne	Rhône
St.-Étienne	Maison Dorée
St.-Just-en-Chevalet	Moderne
PUY-DE-DÔME	
Aigueperse	Crovetto
Ardes-sur-Couze	Dufour
Aydat	Lac
Besse-en-Chandesse	Beffevi
Ceyrat	Poste
Châteldon	Castel Ondon
Effiat	Chât. de Denone
Champeix	Centre
Châtel-Guyon	Gourmets
Fades (Viaduc des)	Chaffraix
Lac Chambon	Chalet du Lac
Pontaumur	Lyon
Pont-de-Dore	Rigoulet
Puy-de-Dôme	Temple de Mercure
Puy-Guillaume	Larivaut
Riom	Grand Hotel
Royat	Belle Meunière
St.-Nectaire	Moderne
Thiers	Du Breuil
CREUSE	
Chénérailles	Poulet
Crocq	Touriste
Évaux-les-Bains	Chardonnet
Felletin	Lozes
Gouzon	Beaune
Gueret	Petit Vatel
St.-Étienne-de-Fursac	Moderne

APPENDIX A

TOWN	HOUSE
HAUTE-VIENNE	
Aix-sur-Vienne	Charente
le Dorat	France
Limoges	Lion d'Or
Rochechouart	Commerce
CHARENTE	
Angoulême	Trois Piliers
Barbezieux	Boule d'Or
Cognac	Londres
Confolens	Bourdier
CHARENTE	
la Rochefoucauld	Grand Hotel
Ruffec	France
CHARENTE-INFÉRIEURE	
Fouras	Chaigneau
Pons	Bordeaux
Rochefort-sur-Mer	Brasserie Continentale
la Rochelle	Henry
St.-Pierre-d'Oleron	Renaissance
Saintes	Terminus
GIRONDE	
Arcachon	Etchea
Bolin	Des Pins
Langon	Oliver
Libourne	Orléans
DORDOGNE	
Brantôme	Chavrol
Monpazier	Londres
Sarlat	Madeleine
Vitrac	Plaisance
CORRÈZE	
Rive	Chapon Fin
Égletons	Bordeaux
St.-Privat	Condamine
Treignac	France
Tulle	Fournaud
Uzerche	**Chavant**

APPENDIX A

TOWN	HOUSE
CANTAL	
Laveissière	Bellevue
Pierrefort	Vidal et Voyageurs
HAUTE-LOIRE	
Craponne-sur-Arzon	Esquis
le Puy	Royal
Sanges	France
ISÈRE	
les Abrets	**Cuaz**
Balme-les-Grottes	**Savoyard-et-Grottes**
Bourgoin	**Besancon**
Laffrey	Humblot
Montalieu-Vercien	**Delauge**
Rives-sur-Fure	**Durand**
Sassenage	Parendel
Uriage-les-Bains	Trianon
Villard-de-Lans	Splendide
Vinay	Parc et Moderne
Voiron	Poste
Vienne	**Pyramide**
SAVOIE	
Aigueblanche	**Perret**
Chambéry	**Maison du Tourisme**
la Chambotte	La Chambotte
Lanslebourg	Valloire
Bourg-St.-Maurice	Pont St.-Bernard
Hautecombe	Abbaye
Lépin	**Chalet du Lac**
Mercury-Gemilly	Beauséjour
St.-Bernard (Col du Petit)	Lancebranlette
St.-Paul-sur-Isère	Grand Arch
Val-d'Isère	**Parisien**
HAUTES-ALPES	
St.-Julien-en-Beauchêne	Bermond
DRÔME	
Baraques-en-Vercors	Midi
Livron	**Voyageurs**

APPENDIX A

TOWN	HOUSE
DRÔME – *continued*	
Lus-la-Croix-Haute	Touring
Montélimar	Relais de l'Empereur
Pierrelatte	Host. Pierrelatte
Pont-de-Manne	**Pont-de-Manne**
St.-Jean-en-Royans	Royans
Tain-l'Hermitage	Hermitage
Valence-sur-Rhône	Europe
ARDÈCHE	
Annonay	Chatain
Alboussière	Pic
le Cheylard	Midi
Lalouvesc	Mon Besset
Lamastre	Midi
la Voultre-sur-Rhône	Rhône
St.-Agrève	Jouve
LOZÈRE	
la Bastide	Terminus
la Malène	Commerce
AVEYRON	
Decazeville	France
Entraygues	Lion d'Or
Rodez	**Broussy**
St.-Jean-du-Bruel	Papillon
Villefranche-de-Rouergue	Colombes
LOT	
Alvignac	Branche Lescure
Cabrerets	Touristes
Cahors	**Ambassadeurs**
Concots	Voyageurs
Figeac	Moderne et Voyageurs
Lacave	Grottes
Padirac	Gouffre
Payrac	Host. Paix
Presque (Grotte de)	Superpresque
Rocamadour	Ste.-Marie
St.-Céré	Touring-Hotel

APPENDIX A

TOWN	HOUSE
LOT-ET-GARONNE	
Agen	Festal
Casteljaloux	Grand Hôtel Fages
Ste.-Bazeille	Rebeyrol
Villeneuve-sur-Lot	Gache
Villeréal	Commerce
LANDES	
Grenades-sur-l'Adour	France
Hossegor	Lac
Mont-de-Marsan	Richelieu
Pissoss	Commerce
St.-Sever	France
St.-Vincent-de-Tyrosse	Voyageurs
Tartas	Mallet
GERS	
Lectoure	France
TARN-ET-GARONNE	
Beaumont-de-Lomagne	Commerce
Castelsarrasin	Moderne
Caussade	Larroque
Montauban	Midi
TARN	
Albi	Puech
Cordes	Vieux Cordes
Lacaune	Central
Lavaur	Moderne
HÉRAULT	
Agde	Midi
Béziers	Chapon Fin
Caylar	Larzac
Ganges	Croix Blanche
Lamalou-les-Bains	Paix
Lodève	Nord
Montpellier	Brasserie Modérne
Palavas-les-Flots	Flots-Bleus
Sète	Grand Café

APPENDIX A

TOWN	HOUSE
GARD	
Alès	Évêché
Baume	Host. de la Baume
Le-Grau-du-Roi	Café Continental
Nîmes	Castanet
Uzès	L'Oustalou
Villeneuve-les-Avignon	Midi
VAUCLUSE	
Avignon	Hiély
Carpentras	Brasserie Avon
Châteauneuf-du-Pape	Bellevue
Gordes	Pantaly-Gentil (Renaissance)
Mont-Ventoux	Mont-Ventoux
Vaucluse	Jardin de Pétrarque
BASSES-ALPES	
Digne	Grand Paris
Moustier-Ste.-Marie	Belvedere
Rougon	Pointe-de-Vue
Volonne	Touring
ALPES-MARITIMES	
Antibes	Félix
Beaulieu	Reserve
Grasse	Bianchi
Mandelieu	Provence
Menton	Amiraute
Plan-du-Var	Cassini
Pont-du-Loup	Pont-du-Loup
St.-Jean-Cap-Ferrat	Caramello
St.-Paul	Colombe d'Or
la Turbie	Righi d'Hiver
VAR	
Bormes	La Korrigane
Brignoles	Tivoli
Carqueiranne	Beau Rivage
Cavalière	Grand Hôtel
le Rayol	La Réserve

APPENDIX A

TOWN	HOUSE
VAR – *continued*	
St.-Tropez	Bailli
Sanary	Hiély
Toulon	Au Sourd
BOUCHES-DU-RHÔNE	
Arles	Vauxhall
Ciotat	Golf
Rognac	Royal Provence
Roquefavour	De l'Arquier
Tholonet	Thomé
AUDE	
Carcassonne	Auter
Castelnaudary	Grand Hotel
HAUTE-GARONNE	
Antichan-de-Frontignes	Des Frontignes
Bagnères-de-Luchon	Charmilles
St.-Gaudens	Comminges
Toulouse	Lucullus
PYRÉNÉES-ORIENTALES	
Canet-Plage	Beau Rivage
Perpignan	Lion d'Or
Port-Vendres	Cie du Midi
Vernet-les-Bains	Termes
ARIÈGE	
Foix	XIXe Siècle
Mirepoix	Commerce
St.-Girons	Eychenne
HAUTES-PYRÉNÉES	
Bagnères-de-Bigorre	Bigorre
Cauterets	Bonne Auberge
Maubourguet	St.-Germain et France
Tarbes	Moderne
BASSES-PYRÉNÉES	
Betharram	Des Grottes
Biarritz	Guillot
Itxassou	Pas de Roland
Louvie-Juzon	Dhérété

APPENDIX A

TOWN	HOUSE
BASSE-PYRÉNÉES – *continued*	
Mauléon-Licharre	Bidegain
Pau	Pierre
Orthez	Belle-Hôtesse
St.-Jean-de-Luz	Ciboure
St.-Étienne-de-Baigorry	Pyrénées
Salies-de-Bearn	Pavillon Médici
MOSELLE	
Metz	Moitrier
Sierck	Grégoire
Vic-sur-Seille	Voizard
BAS-RHIN	
Stambach	Fameuse Truite
HAUT-RHIN	
Aubure	Brézouard
Colmar	Maison des Têtes
Kaysersberg	**Chambard**
Masevaux	Aigle d'Or
Moosch	France
Thann	Parc

APPENDIX (B)

SCALE OF FRENCH INCOME-TAX (to the nearest franc)

		MARRIED		
Income (frs.)	Single person (a).	For less than 2 years (b).	With one child under 21 or infirm.	With two children under 21 or infirm.
7000	—	—	—	—
10,000	36	—	—	—
15,000	96	60	23	—
20,000	156	120	81	41
25,000	276	204	137	97
30,000	396	324	239	162
35,000	576	468	353	270
40,000	756	648	513	389
45,000	996	852	684	551
50,000	1236	1092	901	723
55,000	1536	1356	1129	940
60,000	1836	1656	1402	1177
65,000	2196	1980	1687	1436
70,000	2556	2340	2018	1717
75,000	2976	2724	2360	2041
80,000	3396	3144	2747	2376
85,000	3876	3588	3148	2754
90,000	4356	4068	3591	3143
95,000	4896	4572	4247	3575
100,000	5436	5112	4549	4018
110,000	6636	6276	5620	5000
120,000	7836	7476	6760	6080
130,000	9096	8700	7900	7160
140,000	10,416	10,020	9142	8305

T

APPENDIX B

		MARRIED		
Income (frs.)	Single person (a).	For less than 2 years (b).	With one child under 21 or infirm.	With two children under 21 or infirm.
150,000	11,736	11,340	10,397	9493
160,000	13,176	12,744	11,696	10,692
170,000	14,616	14,184	13,064	11,988
180,000	16,116	15,648	14,432	13,284
190,000	17,676	17,208	15,903	14,645
200,000	19,236	18,768	17,385	16,049
210,000	20,916	20,412	18,913	17,464
220,000	22,596	22,092	20,509	19,976
230,000	24,336	23,796	22,105	22,488
240,000	26,136	25,596	23,803	22,064

I have not continued this scale beyond the £2000 a year income — assumed upon a rental of about £286 per annum. The figures are those of the 1928 Budget.

(a) Plus 25 per cent. if the taxpayer is over 30 years of age.

(b) Plus 10 per cent. if the taxpayer is over 30 years and has been married two years.

APPENDIX (C)

TAX ON MOTOR-CARS (1930 Budget).

The State Tax and the Municipal Tax are here compounded, only the approximate total being given. The Municipal Tax varies slightly according to the municipality, but the difference to the total is not great: certain departments add a small departmental tax. The figures quoted are for three months.

H.P. (Fr.)	Tax (frs.)	H.P.(Fr.)	Tax (frs.)	H.P.(Fr.)	Tax (frs.)
5	105	17	458	29	885
6	132	18	490	30	921
7	178	19	521	31	964
8	184	20	553	32	1005
9	211	21	590	33	1048
10	237	22	627	34	1080
11	269	23	663	35	1132
12	300	24	700	36	1174
13	332	25	737	37	1216
14	363	26	774	38	1258
15	395	27	811	39	1300
16	426	28	848	40	1343

INDEX

OF PLACES MENTIONED

A

Abbeville, 36
Agde, 154
Agen, 159
Aigues-Mortes, 105
Aix-en-Provence, 81
Albi, 159
Annot, 102
Arcachon, 203
Arles, 150
Arnay-le-Duc, 117
Arras, 132
Auch, 158
Autun, 118
Auxerre, 122
Avallon, 117
Avignon, 75

B

Balaguier, 140
Bandol, 146
Beaulieu, 95
Beaune, 119
Beauvais, 38-40
Belley, 107, 108
Besançon, 130

Béziers, 155
Bordeaux, 199-204
Boulogne, 28-33
Bourg, 111, 112
Bourges, 56

C

Cahors, 164
Calais, 27
Cannes, 87-90
Cap d'Antibes, 90
Carcassonne, 157
Carry-le-Rouet, 197
Cassis, 146
Castellane, 104
Castres, 164
Caussade, 164
Cavaillon, 79
Chagny, 115, 116
Chalon-sur-Saône, 115
Charbonnières-les-Bains, 185
la Charité-sur-Loire, 58
Charolles, 60
Chartres, 49
Châteauneuf-du-Pape, 74
Châteauneuf-sur-Loire, 50
la Clayette, 60, 61

INDEX

Clermont-Ferrand, 64, 65
Cluny, 118
Colmar, 131
Comarin, 121
Condom, 158
Crécy, 36

D

Dieppe, 25
Digne, 105
Dijon, 119, 21
Draguignan, 185

E

Evreux, 171, 172

F

Fontainebleau, 123, 126
Fréjus, 84
Freteval, 170
Frontignan, 154

G

Gemenos, 147
Gisors, 46
Gordes, 78
Grandvilliers, 37
Grasse, 103
le Grau-du-Roi, 151
Grenoble, 107
Grimaldi, 100

H

Havre, 25

J

Joinville, 129
Juan-les-Pins, 90

K

Kaysersberg, 131

L

Lamalou, 163
Lambesc, 81
les Lèques, 146
Lodève, 162
Loriol, 70
Louhans, 182
le Luc-en-Diois, 107
le Luc-en-Provence, 83
Luxeuil, 131
Lyon, 175-185

M

Mâcon, 65
Manosque, 79
Mantes, 46
Marseille, 186-198
Marseille-en-Beauvaisis, 37
Martigues, 149

INDEX

Martin-Église, 173
Menton, 97-99
Méounes, 144
Monestier-de-Clermont, 106
Monte Carlo, 95-97
Montélimar, 71-73
Montpellier, 152, 153
Montreuil-le-Vieux, 144
Montreuil-sur-Mer, 35

N

Nancy, 129
Napont, 35
Narbonne, 157
Nice, 91, 92
Nîmes, 151
Nogent-sur-Vernisson, 54, 55
Nolay, 116
Nonancourt, 171
Nouvion, 36

O

Orange, 73

P

Palavas, 154
Paris, 41
les Pins-de-Galles, 141
Pithiviers, 53
Poitiers, 166-169
Poix, 37
Pougues-les-Eaux, 58
Pouilly-sur-Loire, 57
Puget-Théniers, 102
Précy-sous-Thil, 118

R

Rambouillet, 47
Reims, 132
Roanne, 63
Robinson, 45
la Rochepot, 122
les Roches Rouges, 100
Rougon, 80

S

St.-André-les-Alpes, 103
St.-Germain-en-Laye, 43
St.-Jean-Cap-Ferrat, 92-95
St.-Jean-en-Beauchêne, 106
St.-Pons, 159
St.-Raphael, 136
Ste.-Baume, 147
Salon, 148
Samer, 34
Sanary, 145
Saulieu, 116
Saumur, 170
Sens, 122
la Seyne, 140
Sisteron, 106
Soissons, 131
Sorgues, 75
Strasbourg, 129, 130

T

Tain, 69
Thiers, 63

INDEX

Tholonet, 82
Tonneins, 159
Toulon, 137-139
Toulouse, 157, 158
Troyes, 128

U

Uzerche, 165

V

Valence, 69
Versailles, 44
Vidauban, 84
Vichy, 59
Vienne, 67-69
Volonne, 105

CPSIA information can be obtained
at www.ICGtesting.com
Printed in the USA
LVHW031419040220
645647LV00001B/59

9 781846 646522